Crossing The Gap:

Your Ultimate Path to Financial Freedom

Carson Manuel

Copyright © by Carson Manuel 2024. All rights reserved.
No portion of 'Crossing The Gap: Your Ultimate Path to Financial Freedom' may be duplicated or transmitted in any form without the author's prior written consent. Unauthorized replication is strictly banned and may result in legal consequences. Join us on the path to recovering your wealth and well-being, but please appreciate the time and effort that went into developing this transformative guide.

Table of Contents

Foreword 2
Introduction 4
Chapter 1: Define Financial Freedom 6
   1.1 What is financial freedom? 6
   1.2 Why Strive for Financial Freedom? 7
   1.3 Benefits of Financial Independence 9
Chapter 2: Assessment of Your Current Financial Situation 12
   2.1 Understand Your Financial Health 12
   2.2 Evaluate Your Assets and Liabilities 14
   2.3 Calculate Your Net Worth 16
Chapter 3: Identifying Financial Goals 20
   3.1 Set SMART Financial Goals 20
   3.2 Short-Term Versus Long-Term Goals 22
   3.3 Aligning Your Goals and Values 25
Chapter 4: Budgeting and Cash Flow Management 28
   4.1 Setting Up a Personal Budget 28
   4.2 Tracking Expenses 31
   4.3 Cash Management Strategies 33
Chapter 5: Debt Management and Elimination 36
   5.1 Understanding Different Types of Debt 36
   5.2 Establish a Debt Repayment Plan 39
   5.3 Tips for Accelerating Debt Repayment 41
Chapter 6: Emergency Funding and Risk Management 44
   6.1: The Importance of an Emergency Fund 44
   6.2 Establishing and Maintaining Your Emergency Fund 47
   6.3 Insurance Planning for Financial Security 49

Chapter 7: An Introduction to Investing ... 52
7.1 Investment Fundamentals and Principles ... 52
7.2: Understanding Risk and Return ... 54

Chapter 8: Create an Investment Portfolio ... 58
8.1 Asset Allocation Strategy ... 58
8.2 Diversification Techniques ... 60
8.3 Investment Vehicles and Option ... 63

Chapter 9: Retirement Planning. ... 66
9.1 Set Retirement Goals ... 66
9.2 Retirement Account Options (401k, IRA, etc.) ... 68
9.3 Strategy for Retirement Savings ... 71

Chapter 10: Real Estate Investment ... 74
10.1 Real Estate Investment Basics ... 74
10.2 Rental Properties vs. Real Estate Investment Trusts (REITs) ... 77
10.3 Maximizing Returns on Real Estate ... 80

Chapter 11: Entrepreneurship and Passive Income ... 84
11.1 Starting and Scaling Your Business ... 84
11.2 Generate Passive Income Streams ... 87
11.3 Managing Risks and Rewards in Entrepreneurship ... 90

Chapter 12: Tax Planning and Optimization. ... 94
12.1: Understanding tax laws and regulations ... 94
12.2 Tax-Efficient Investing Strategy ... 97
12.3: Reducing Tax Liabilities for Long-Term Wealth ... 99

Chapter 13: Overcoming Financial Setbacks ... 104
13.1 Strategies for Recovering from Financial Hardships ... 104
13.2 Strengthening Resilience in the Face of Adversity ... 106
13.3 Seeking Professional Help as Needed ... 108

Chapter 14: Economic Change and Market Volatility 112

14.1 Adapting to Economic Changes 112

14.2 Thriving Under Volatile Market Conditions 114

14.3 Investment Strategy for Uncertain Times 116

Chapter 15: Lifestyle Design and Personal Fulfillment. 120

15.1: Define Your Ideal Lifestyle 120

15.2 Balancing Financial Goals and Personal Values 122

15.3 Promoting Happiness and Well-Being Beyond Money 124

Chapter 16: Giving Back and Legacy Planning 128

16.1 The Importance of Giving Back 128

16.2 Plan Your Legacy and Impact 130

16.3 Building a Lasting Financial Legacy 132

Conclusion 136

Glossary 138

Foreword

Navigating the complexities of money management can often seem like a daunting task in the world of personal finance. There are many obstacles, unknowns, and possibilities on the path to financial well-being, from investing and budgeting to retirement planning and beyond. We set out on a trip together in this preface, where we will examine the ideas and methods that can provide you with more power over your financial destiny and lead to long-term wealth. Fundamentally, developing financial stamina is about creating a strong foundation for a life of stability, independence, and fulfillment rather than merely amassing cash. It's about making deliberate decisions that are in line with your values and objectives and realizing the potential of money as a tool for building the life you want. These books' concepts will be your road map to success, whether your goal is to pay off debt, invest your way into riches, or ensure a happy retirement. You'll discover helpful guidance, doable tactics, and insightful information on the pages that follow to enable you to confidently negotiate the complexity of personal finance. With each chapter covering topics such as retirement planning, investing, and budgeting, as well as how to define financial freedom and set meaningful objectives, you will gain the knowledge and abilities necessary to succeed in the constantly shifting world of finance today. However, developing the proper mindset and attitude toward wealth is just as important as learning the technical components of money management if you want to build financial stamina. It's about adopting an abundant, resourceful, and resilient mindset that enables you to overcome barriers, adjust to setbacks, and grasp chances for development and success. I urge you to approach the process with an open mind and a desire to learn and develop as you set out on this trip. Recall that achieving financial success is a continual process of personal development and exploration rather than a final goal. You'll face uncertainties, difficulties, and setbacks along the way, but how you handle these setbacks will ultimately define how successful you are. I also urge you to embark on this adventure with an open mind and an exploratory mindset. Take the time to investigate novel concepts, try out novel tactics, and look for chances for development and advancement. Never be scared to seek advice from professionals, ask questions, and make mistakes to learn from them. A lifetime learning and continual

improvement mindset can help you reach your financial objectives and successfully negotiate the challenges of personal finance. Lastly, I would like to recognize that developing financial resilience is a group effort as much as an individual one. To keep you accountable, inspired, and focused on your financial journey, it's about creating a community of support. Surround yourself with people who share your aims and values and who can offer direction, support, and encouragement along the road, whether it's through family, friends, mentors, or online networks. I'd like to thank you for starting the process of developing financial stamina. You've already made a big step toward reaching your objectives and building the life you want by taking up this book and making a commitment to your financial well-being. With any luck, the advice and techniques in these pages will encourage and enable you to take charge of your money, get past setbacks, and enjoy long-term success. Keep in mind that while achieving financial stamina is not always simple, it is worthwhile. Cheers to your riches and happiness!
Sincerely,
Carson Manuel

Introduction

There once lived a young woman named Emma in a bustling city tucked between tall towers and meandering streets. Emma had the same bright eyes, aspirations, and desire to take on the world as many of her contemporaries. Emma had a bright façade, but underlying that was a secret yearning for something more than the grind of everyday life in the concrete jungle. Emma made a decision that night that would change her life forever. She was sitting at her messy desk in her little apartment, surrounded by piles of bills and a growing sense of financial anxiety. She made the resolve to set out on a mission: the pursuit of financial independence. Emma found that the route to financial freedom was not a clear-cut path but rather a convoluted one with many detours and unanticipated obstacles as she continued on her trip. She came across a group of people who would influence how she saw money, riches, and what it truly meant to be abundant. Mr. Thompson was an old man Emma met for the first time on her travels. Mr. Thompson was an experienced and knowledgeable investor who had navigated the turbulent stock market for his entire life. He enthralled Emma with stories of market booms and collapses over lengthy talks and hot coffee in dimly lit cafes, instilling in her the values of perseverance, caution, and sticking to the course in the face of uncertainty. Emma then met Maria, a dynamic businesswoman who had a love for starting companies from scratch. Maria had an endless supply of energy and contagious enthusiasm as she divulged her insider knowledge on how to succeed in the business world, from identifying profitable prospects to gracefully and resiliently weathering setbacks and disappointments. Emma continued her travels and met James, a kind man who worked as a modest janitor and had quietly saved up a tiny fortune via thrift, hard work, and compound interest. James led an abundant life despite his meager circumstances, finding contentment and satisfaction in the small pleasures of community, friendship, and family. Emma's awareness of wealth and plenty grew with every day, and she came to understand that true financial freedom was a state of mind that transcended worldly money—an attitude of abundance, thankfulness, and generosity—rather than just a goal to be achieved. Equipped with acquired knowledge and a revitalized sense of direction, Emma persevered, surmounting hindrances and difficulties with bravery and tenacity. Over time, she discovered that genuine wealth was determined by the depth of her connections, the richness of her experiences, and the difference she made in the world rather than the amount of money in her bank account. As a result, she learned to appreciate life's ups and downs. Thus, I cordially encourage you to accompany Emma on her journey of self-realization, development, and metamorphosis. You will discover timeless truths and priceless lessons along the way that will enable you to forge your path to financial independence and build a life that exceeds your wildest expectations in terms of prosperity, joy, and fulfillment. Because achieving financial freedom is a journey rather than a destination, one filled with opportunity, adventure, and unending discovery, may you, upon starting this journey, discover the strength to follow your intuition, the discernment to meet obstacles head-on, and the faith that everything is possible when you dare to dream big and pursue your passions with unflinching dedication. Greetings from the path to monetary independence. There's an adventure ahead.

Chapter 1: Define Financial Freedom

Few notions in personal finance offer as much attraction and promise as financial independence. It is a phrase that is often used in debates about money and wealth, but what exactly does it mean? What is financial independence, and why is it so important in the lives of so many people?

1.1 What is financial freedom?

Financial freedom is defined as being free of financial anxieties, restraints, and limits. It is the opportunity to make decisions and live life on your terms, unhindered by financial responsibilities or limitations. However, financial independence entails more than just possessing a huge bank account or owning significant assets. It's about having control over your financial situation and the freedom to follow your goals and desires without being hampered by money worries.

At its essence, financial independence is about having choices. It is the freedom to decide how you spend your time, where you live, what you do for a living, and how you contribute to society. It is about having the means to sustain yourself and your loved ones now and in the future without having to depend on others for financial aid.

Financial independence looks different for each person since it is determined by their values, priorities, and aspirations. Some individuals may see it as an opportunity to retire early and tour the globe. Others may consider establishing a company, working on a passion project, or spending more time with family and friends. Finally, financial independence means having the power to create a life that is consistent with your beliefs and provides you with joy and happiness.

Achieving financial independence involves meticulous preparation, discipline, and dedication. It entails establishing a sound financial foundation, managing debt responsibly, and accumulating wealth through savings and investment. It also requires making sound financial decisions and being prepared to modify and amend your goals when circumstances change.

However, financial independence is more than merely collecting money or attaining a certain salary level. It's also important to have a positive connection with money and create an abundant attitude. It's about being appreciative of what you have and making deliberate decisions that promote your long-term financial well-being.

In essence, financial independence is about getting control of your financial situation so that you can concentrate on what is genuinely important to you. It is about achieving peace of mind and security by knowing that you have the resources and freedom to live the life you want. Perhaps most significantly, it is about realizing that genuine riches are found not in money and stuff but in the capacity to live a meaningful and full life on your terms.

1.2 Why Strive for Financial Freedom?

As we go further into the notion of financial independence, it is critical to investigate the underlying motives and reasons for people embarking on the quest to achieve it. Why do individuals want financial independence, and what motivates them to strive for more control over their finances?

1. Pursuit of Independence

A desire for independence is one of the key reasons people want financial freedom. Financial independence allows people to make decisions that are consistent with their beliefs and ambitions without relying on others for financial assistance. It frees individuals from the confines of living paycheck to paycheck or being forced to work at a job they despise only for financial reasons. Individuals with financial freedom can follow their interests, take risks, and explore new possibilities without worrying about financial instability.

2. Safety and peace of mind

Another powerful motive for wanting financial independence is the need for stability and peace of mind. Financial independence protects against life's uncertainties, such as unforeseen costs, job losses, or economic downturns. It enables people to weather financial storms with confidence, knowing they have enough resources to maintain themselves and their families during difficult times. Furthermore, financial independence reduces the stress and worry that comes with money problems, enabling people to concentrate on other elements of their lives, including health, relationships, and personal development.

3. Fulfillment and Personal Development

Financial independence allows people to completely follow their hobbies and interests. It enables individuals to invest in their personal and professional growth, seek lifelong learning opportunities, and participate in activities that offer them contentment and joy. Whether it's touring the globe, establishing a company, or volunteering for a cause they care about, financial independence allows people to live life to the fullest and realize their full potential. Furthermore, pursuing financial independence often entails defining and completing objectives, which promotes a feeling of success and personal development along the journey.

4. Legacy and generational wealth

For many people, the search for financial independence goes beyond their immediate wants and ambitions. It's about leaving a legacy and creating generational wealth that will benefit their families and communities for years to come. Individuals who achieve financial independence may leave a lasting legacy for future generations, offering chances and resources that enable their loved ones to grow and prosper. Whether it's paying for education for children and grandchildren, supporting charity organizations, or leaving a meaningful legacy, financial independence enables people to have a lasting impact on the world.

5. Freedom of choice and lifestyle design

Finally, financial independence means having the flexibility to live a life consistent with one's beliefs, objectives, and goals. It's about having the freedom to choose how you spend your time, where you live, and what interests you choose to pursue without being limited by finances. Whether it's retiring early, following a passion project, or traveling the globe, financial independence allows people to live life on their terms and establish a lifestyle that provides them pleasure and satisfaction.

To summarize, the quest for financial freedom is motivated by several motives, including a desire for independence, stability, satisfaction, legacy, and freedom of choice. It's a path that needs commitment, discipline, and endurance, but the rewards—both physical and intangible—are well worth it. Individuals who want financial independence may open up a world of possibilities and live a life that matches their core beliefs and objectives.

1.3 Benefits of Financial Independence

Understanding the advantages of financial independence is critical to the path to financial freedom. Financial independence, also known as financial freedom, is a situation in which people have collected enough money and resources to support their preferred lifestyle without depending on outside sources of income. Let's look at the many advantages of achieving financial independence and how it may significantly improve people's lives.

1. Peace of Mind and Less Stress

One of the most important advantages of financial independence is the peace of mind it provides. Knowing you have a strong financial foundation and the resources to pay your bills gives you a feeling of security and decreases stress. Financially independent people are less likely to be concerned about job losses, economic downturns, or unanticipated bills since they have the financial resources to weather such problems without altering their lifestyles.

2. The freedom to pursue passion and purpose

Individuals with financial independence have the opportunity to pursue their interests and purposes without being constrained by financial restraints. Whether it's establishing a company, touring the globe, or donating time to charitable causes, financial freedom allows you to devote your time and resources to things that offer you pleasure and contentment. It enables people to match their lives with their beliefs and goals, resulting in a better feeling of fulfillment and purpose.

3. Flexibility and autonomy

Financial independence gives people more freedom and autonomy in their lives. Financially independent individuals can establish their schedules, follow alternative career routes, or explore non-conventional work arrangements such as freelancing or remote work since they are not required to rely on a continuous salary or conform to typical employment structures. This flexibility allows people to achieve a better work-life balance and adjust their lifestyle to their interests.

4. Able to Retire Early

One of the most sought-after advantages of financial freedom is the chance to retire early and live a leisurely lifestyle. Individuals who accumulate enough money and passive income streams might opt to retire from regular work at a younger age and devote their time to hobbies, travel, or just rest. Early retirement helps people recover their time and enjoy the results of their efforts while they are still young and healthy, resulting in a more rewarding retirement.

5. Increased financial security for future generations

Financial freedom helps both people and future generations. Individuals who achieve financial independence may leave a legacy for their family and loved ones while also providing a secure future for themselves. Whether it's supporting schooling for children and grandchildren, caring for elderly parents, or leaving an inheritance, financial independence allows people to leave a legacy and assist their loved ones for generations to come.

6. Increased control over life decisions

Perhaps one of the most powerful benefits of financial independence is the increased control it provides over life choices. Financially independent individuals have the freedom to make decisions that are consistent with their beliefs and aims because they are not bound by financial responsibilities or the need to earn a living. Whether it's moving to a new location, establishing a new business, or taking a sabbatical to explore personal interests, financial independence gives you the flexibility to negotiate life's changes with confidence and conviction.

7. Increased mental and emotional well-being

Finally, financial independence may help enhance mental and emotional health. According to research, financial stress is a major factor in anxiety, depression, and other mental health problems. Individuals who achieve financial independence and reduce financial stress might have more overall pleasure, life satisfaction, and peace of mind. Financial independence allows people to concentrate on what is genuinely important in life, which fosters a feeling of happiness and fulfillment.

Finally, financial independence provides many far-reaching advantages, including not just financial stability but also freedom, flexibility, and personal satisfaction. Individuals who strive for financial independence may open up a new universe of possibilities and construct a life that represents their innermost beliefs and goals.

Chapter 2: Assessment of Your Current Financial Situation

Navigating the route to financial independence demands a thorough awareness of one's existing financial situation. The second chapter delves into the critical process of reviewing your current financial situation, which starts with knowing your financial health.

2.1 Understand Your Financial Health

Consider your financial health to be a snapshot of your total financial well-being, including all of your financial assets, obligations, income, spending, and savings practices. Just like a doctor evaluates a patient's health before prescribing medication, it is critical to review your financial health to identify areas of strength and places for development.

Financial health indicators

Assessing your financial health entails looking at several important factors that provide insight into your financial well-being:

1. Money: Consider your sources of money, such as earnings, salaries, bonuses, investments, and any other sources of revenue. Consider whether your income is consistent, increasing, or changing, as well as whether it meets your financial needs and objectives.

2. Expenditures: Consider your monthly expenditures, which include fixed costs like rent or mortgage payments, utilities, and insurance premiums, as well as variable expenses such as food, entertainment, and discretionary spending. Understanding where your money flows might help you find areas for cost-cutting and budget improvement.

3. Assets: Evaluate your cash reserves, investments, retirement accounts, real estate, and precious things. Consider the liquidity, growth potential, and diversity of your assets to ensure they are in line with your financial objectives and risk tolerance.

4. Obligations: Take stock of your obligations, which include outstanding bills, loans, mortgages, and credit card balances. Examine the interest rates, payback periods, and overall debt load to see how they affect your financial health and cash flow.

5. Savings Rate: Determine your savings rate, which is the proportion of your income you save or invest every month. A good savings rate suggests that you have disciplined financial habits and are working toward your financial objectives, such as saving for retirement or financing large expenditures.

Financial ratios and metrics

In addition to assessing specific financial components, consider utilizing financial ratios and indicators to assess your overall financial health:

1. Debt-to-income ratio: To calculate your debt-to-income ratio, divide your total monthly debt payments by your gross monthly income. A lower debt-to-income ratio suggests more financial stability.

2. Savings Rate: As previously stated, your savings rate is the percentage of your income that you save or invest. Aim for a savings rate that permits you to satisfy your immediate financial demands while still developing long-term wealth.

3. Net Worth: To calculate your net worth, subtract your entire liabilities from your total assets. Your net worth gives a comprehensive picture of your financial situation and serves as a baseline for measuring growth over time.

4. Emergency Fund Coverage: Determine your emergency fund's size by comparing it to your monthly expenses. To defend against unforeseen financial losses, have an emergency fund of three to six months' worth of living costs on hand.

Financial health checkup

Now that you've learned the basic financial health markers and measures, it's time to do a financial health exam. Begin by collecting your financial papers, such as bank statements, investment account statements, credit card statements, and loan statements.

Next, utilize budgeting tools, spreadsheets, or financial software to arrange your financial data and compute key ratios and KPIs. Be honest and comprehensive in your evaluation, and do not be afraid to seek assistance from financial experts or specialists if necessary.

Finally, analyze the findings of your financial health exam to discover areas for improvement. Create practical plans and objectives to address any deficiencies while capitalizing on positives, such as boosting income, lowering costs, paying off debt, or increasing savings contributions.

Remember that analyzing your financial health is a continuous process that needs constant monitoring and modification. Understanding your financial status and taking proactive efforts to improve it may help you build a firm foundation for reaching financial independence and living the life you want.

2.2 Evaluate Your Assets and Liabilities

While pursuing financial independence, understanding your financial situation is critical. Chapter 2 goes into the crucial process of assessing your assets and obligations, offering information about your present financial situation, and building the framework for educated decision-making.

Understanding assets

Assets are financial resources that can be transformed into cash. They reflect your financial strength and add to your total net worth. Evaluating your assets entails identifying, classifying, and determining the worth and liquidity of each item.

Asset Types:

1. Cash and Cash Equivalents: This category includes cash on hand, savings accounts, checking accounts, money market accounts, and certificates of deposit (CDs). Cash and cash equivalents are extremely liquid and readily available for short-term financial needs.

2. Investments: Investments include a variety of financial instruments such as equities, bonds, mutual funds, exchange-traded funds (ETFs), retirement accounts (401(k), IRAs), and real estate investment trusts (REITs). Investments have the possibility for growth and income, but they differ in terms of risk and liquidity.

3. Real Estate: Real estate assets include primary dwellings, rental properties, vacation houses, and commercial real estate. Real estate may offer rental income, capital appreciation, and tax advantages, but it may need constant care and supervision.

4. Company interests: Owning a company or having stock in a business endeavor is a significant asset. Business interests may create income, dividends, and capital gains, but they can also be risky and fluctuate in value.

5. Personal Property: Personal property includes assets such as automobiles, jewelry, art, collections, furniture, and other monetary items. Personal property increases your net worth, yet it may not provide income or increase in value over time.

Assessing liabilities

Liabilities, on the other hand, are the financial responsibilities or debts that you owe creditors or lenders. Evaluating your liabilities entails identifying, classifying, and comprehending the terms, interest rates, and payback requirements related to each one.

Various types of liabilities:

1. Mortgages: Mortgage loans are secured debts used to fund the acquisition of real estate, such as residences or investment properties. Mortgages often have fixed or variable interest rates and demand long-term payments.

2. Consumer Debt: Consumer debt is defined as credit card balances, personal loans, auto loans, and other types of unsecured debt used to fund goods or costs. Consumer debt often has higher interest rates and shorter payback durations than mortgages.

3. Student Loans: Student loans are debts used to cover higher education expenditures such as tuition, fees, books, and living expenses. Student loans may have fixed or variable interest rates, as well as a variety of repayment and forgiveness alternatives.

4. Vehicle Loans: Vehicle loans are installment loans used to fund the purchase of automobiles, trucks, or other vehicles. Vehicle loans often feature fixed interest rates and demand monthly payments over a certain period.

5. Other Liabilities: Additional liabilities may include medical expenses, tax payments, lines of credit, or business loans. These liabilities differ in size, interest rates, and payback durations, but they all reflect financial commitments that must be handled and paid back over time.

Calculating Net worth

Once you've determined your assets and obligations, determining your net worth is simple. To calculate your net worth, simply subtract your overall obligations from your total assets. A positive net worth shows that your assets outnumber your obligations, while a negative net worth suggests the reverse.

Interpreting the Results and Taking Action

After assessing your assets and liabilities and estimating your net worth, it is critical to analyze the findings and identify areas for development. Consider the steps below:

1. Identify strengths and weaknesses: Determine which assets contribute the most to your net worth and which obligations provide the most financial stress. Determine where you can optimize your asset allocation, minimize debt, or increase cash flow.

2. Set goals and prioritize actions. Determine short- and long-term financial objectives based on your asset and liability assessments. Prioritize activities that are in

line with your objectives, such as building savings, paying off high-interest debt, or investing in income-generating assets.

3. Monitor progress and alter tactics: Monitor your financial situation regularly, keep track of changes in asset values and obligations, and adjust your tactics as needed. Reassess your objectives regularly and adjust your financial plan to reflect any changes in your circumstances or priorities.

Evaluating your assets and obligations provides significant insights into your financial health and positions you for success on the road to financial independence. Understanding where you are now enables you to make educated choices and make proactive efforts toward meeting your financial objectives.

2.3 Calculate Your Net Worth

Understanding your net worth is an important hurdle on your path to financial independence, as it provides insight into your overall financial health and development. Chapter 2 delves into the critical process of measuring your net worth and comprehending what it means for your present financial condition.

What is net worth?

Net worth is a financial term that measures the difference between your total assets and liabilities. In plain words, it is the value that remains after subtracting what you owe from what you possess. Net worth is a measure of your financial situation, reflecting whether you are creating money or acquiring debt over time.

How to Calculate Your Net Worth

Calculating your net worth consists of two steps: first, identify and value your assets and liabilities, and then remove your total liabilities from your total assets.

Step 1: Determine and Value Your Assets

Begin by making a thorough inventory of all of your assets, including cash, investments, real estate, personal property, and business interests. Each asset should be assigned a fair market value based on its current market price. For cash, investments, and real estate, utilize their current balances or market values. Using similar sales or assessment data, estimate the value of personal property and business interests.

Here's an overview of common assets and how to value them:

1. Cash and Cash Equivalents: Include the amounts in your savings, checking, money market, and CD accounts.

2. Investments: Include the market value of stocks, bonds, mutual funds, ETFs, retirement accounts, and other investment assets.

3. Real Estate: Include the current market value of your principal house, rental properties, vacation homes, and any other real estate assets you hold.

4. Personal Property: Consider the worth of automobiles, jewelry, art, collectibles, furniture, electronics, and other precious belongings.

5. Business Interests: Include the total worth of any business ownership holdings, partnerships, or equity investments you possess.

Step 2: Identify and Summarize Your Liabilities

Next, make a list of all your liabilities, which include bills, loans, mortgages, and other financial responsibilities. Take note of each liability's outstanding amount, interest rate, and payback conditions.

Here's an overview of common liabilities:

1. Mortgages: Include the remaining amount on your mortgage loans for principal residences, rental properties, or vacation houses.

2. Consumer Debt: This includes credit card balances, personal loans, vehicle loans, and other types of unsecured debt.

3. Student Loans: Include the outstanding amount on any student loans you have for yourself or your dependents.

4. Vehicle Loans: Include any outstanding balances from loans used to fund the purchase of automobiles.

5. Other Liabilities: This includes medical bills, tax responsibilities, lines of credit, and any other outstanding financial commitments.

Step 3: Calculating Your Net Worth

After you've determined your assets and obligations, it's time to calculate your net worth. To calculate your net worth, subtract all of your obligations from your total assets. The formula for determining net worth is given below:

Net worth is total assets minus total liabilities.

Understanding your net worth

Your net worth provides useful information about your overall financial health and progress toward financial goals. A positive net worth means that your assets outweigh your obligations, indicating financial stability and wealth creation. In contrast, a negative net worth indicates that your obligations exceed your assets, suggesting financial weakness and a possible debt load.

Using Your Net Worth as a Financial Benchmark

Your net worth acts as a reference point for tracking your financial success over time. Regularly monitor and track changes in your net worth to assess the efficacy of your financial strategies and identify areas for improvement. Increase your net worth by accumulating assets, minimizing obligations, and making sound financial choices that are consistent with your long-term objectives.

Conclusion

Calculating your net worth is an essential step in analyzing your present financial condition and building a path to financial independence. Understanding your net worth and using it as a financial benchmark allows you to make informed decisions, measure your progress, and eventually meet your financial goals.

Crossing The Gap

Chapter 3: Identifying Financial Goals

Setting specific and attainable financial objectives is critical on the path to financial independence. Chapter 3 looks into the process of determining your financial objectives, beginning with defining SMART goals (specific, measurable, achievable, relevant, and time-bound).

3.1 Set SMART Financial Goals

Financial goals provide direction and purpose, influencing your choices and activities to achieve your objectives. Setting SMART financial goals guarantees that your goals are well-defined, practical, and reachable, paving the way for success on your financial path.

Understanding the SMART Goals:

1. detailed: Your financial objectives should be clear and detailed, with no space for misunderstanding. Describe clearly what you want to do, why it is essential, and how you intend to accomplish it. For example, instead of establishing a generic goal like "save money," be precise by saying, "Save $10,000 for a down payment on a house within two years."

2. Measurable: Your financial objectives should be quantifiable and measurable, enabling you to monitor progress and assess success. Define quantifiable criteria or milestones to track progress toward your objectives. For example, if your objective is to pay off debt, define the specific amount you want to repay and the timetable for doing so.

3. Achievable: Setting ambitious objectives is important, but they should also be within your means and abilities. Consider your financial resources, talents, and limits while defining objectives to ensure they are attainable. To improve achievability and motivation, break down large goals into smaller, more achievable activities.

4. Relevant: Your financial goals should be in line with your values, priorities, and long-term ambitions. Make sure your objectives are relevant and effective since they will contribute to your overall financial well-being and contentment. Avoid creating

objectives based only on external pressures or cultural expectations; instead, prioritize what is most important to you.

5. Time-bound: Establish deadlines or timetables for meeting your financial objectives to instill a feeling of urgency and responsibility. Set specific start and finish dates, as well as interim milestones, to keep you on track and motivated. Time-bound goals help you plan and prioritize work, ensuring progress toward your objectives.

Examples of SMART financial goals:

1. Save for an Emergency Fund: Put $5,000 in a high-yield savings account. Measurable: Monitor monthly savings contributions and account balances. Achievable: Save a percentage of your monthly salary. Important: Ensure financial stability and peace of mind. Time-bound: Achieve the target within 12 months.

2. Pay Off Credit Card Debt: Specific goal: Pay off $10,000 in credit card debt. Measurable: Monitor monthly loan payments and the remaining amount. Achievable: Increase monthly debt payments while eliminating discretionary expenditures. Relevant: Reduce financial stress and enhance your credit score. Time-bound: Pay off debt within 24 months.

3. Invest for Retirement: Specific: Put $500 each month into a retirement account. Measurable: Track investment contributions and account balances. Achievable: Adjust your budget to include funds for retirement savings. Relevant: Establish long-term wealth and financial stability. Time-bound: Keep contributing until retirement age.

4. Save for a Major Purchase: Specifically, save $20,000 for a new vehicle. Measurable: Keep track of your monthly savings progress and overall savings amount. Achievable: Set aside a chunk of your salary only for automobile savings. Relevant: Achieve your transportation objectives without incurring debt. Time-bound: Save enough money to buy a new automobile within 36 months.

5. Invest in Education: Set aside $10,000 for tuition expenditures. Measurable: Track savings contributions and progress toward goals. Achievable: Set up a specific college savings account and donate consistently. Invest in your personal and professional growth. Time-bound: Save enough for tuition within 18 months.

Conclusion

Setting smart financial goals is an essential first step toward financial success and reaching your aspirations. You may achieve financial independence by creating clear, actionable objectives based on the concepts of specificity, measurability, achievement, relevance, and time-bound. Stay dedicated, and focused, and watch as your SMART objectives guide you to a better financial future.

3.2 Short-Term Versus Long-Term Goals

When pursuing financial independence, it is critical to differentiate between short-term and long-term financial objectives. Chapter 3 looks at the importance of both sorts of objectives, how they vary, and how they work together to shape your financial path.

Understanding short-term goals

Short-term financial goals are targets that you want to attain in a relatively short period, usually between a few months and a few years. These objectives often address urgent needs, priorities, and ambitions, resulting in real milestones that contribute to your overall financial health.

Features of Short-Term Goals:
1. Immediacy: Short-term objectives prioritize meeting current financial demands, such as saving for emergencies, paying off debt, or covering anticipated costs.

2. Tangibility: Short-term goals are tangible and detailed, with defined objectives and quantifiable results that can be met quickly.

3. Flexibility: Short-term objectives are flexible and adaptable since they may alter in response to changing circumstances, priorities, or opportunities.

4. Drive: Meeting short-term goals gives you a feeling of success and drive, which reinforces good financial habits and encourages you to work toward bigger goals.

Examples of short-term goals:
1. Create an Emergency Fund: Set aside three to six months' worth of living costs in a high-yield savings account to handle unforeseen financial setbacks.

2. Pay Off Credit Card Debt: Eliminate outstanding credit card balances by raising monthly payments and creating a debt repayment strategy.

3. Create a Budget: Create a monthly budget to monitor income and spending, discover cost-cutting opportunities, and prioritize savings objectives.

4. Save for a trip: Set aside money every month to fund a trip or travel experience in the following six to twelve months.

5. Invest in Continuing Education: Set aside funds for professional development courses, seminars, or certifications to improve abilities and boost job opportunities.

Understanding Long-Term Goals
Long-term financial goals, on the other hand, include objectives that stretch beyond the near future and are often met over a longer period, frequently many years or decades. These objectives represent your overall financial ambitions and vision, leading your choices and activities to long-term success and satisfaction.

Detailed Long-Term Goals:
1. Vision: Long-term objectives represent your overall vision for your financial future, including retirement, homeownership, and financial independence.

2. Persistence: Achieving long-term objectives involves perseverance, devotion, and persistent work over a longer period, which may include modest gains and occasional setbacks.

3. Commitment: Staying on track and overcoming challenges requires a long-term commitment to disciplined financial habits, strategic planning, and sensible decision-making.

4. *Planning: Long-term objectives need thorough planning and foresight, taking into account aspects such as investment strategies, asset allocation, risk management, and contingency plans to reduce possible hazards and optimize performance.

Examples of long-term goals:
1. Retirement Planning: Create a retirement nest fund to support your preferred lifestyle and meet expenditures throughout retirement, taking into account inflation, healthcare costs, and longevity risk.

2. Homeownership: Save for a down payment, buy a main house, or invest in real estate to increase equity and long-term prosperity.

3. Financial Independence: Become financially independent by creating enough passive income streams to support living costs and pursue personal hobbies without depending on conventional work.

4. Education Funding: Save for your child's education expenditures, such as college tuition, by investing in tax-advantaged accounts like 529 plans or Coverdell Education Savings Accounts (ESAs).

5. Legacy Planning: Make a legacy plan to protect wealth, pass assets to heirs, support charity organizations, or leave an indelible mark on future generations.

How to Balance Short-Term and Long-Term Goals

While short-term and long-term objectives serve different functions, they are inextricably linked and impact one another in determining your financial path. Balancing short-term demands with long-term goals involves careful prioritizing, strategic planning, and continuous review to maintain consistency with your overall financial strategy and principles.

Conclusion

Identifying short-term and long-term financial objectives is critical to attaining financial success and accomplishing your aspirations. Setting SMART objectives that meet present demands while also preparing for the future allows you to construct a thorough road map that will lead your financial choices and activities toward long-term wealth and satisfaction. Stay focused and devoted, and see your objectives bring you closer to financial independence.

3.3 Aligning Your Goals and Values

To achieve financial independence, you must verify that your financial objectives are in line with your beliefs and priorities. Chapter 3 discusses the importance of matching your objectives with your values, how to discover your fundamental values and the advantages of pursuing goals that are meaningful to you.

Understanding Value-Based Goal Setting
Values serve as guiding principles for determining what is most essential in your life. They include ideas, values, and ideals that influence your choices, actions, and goals. When defining financial goals, connecting them with your values ensures that your efforts are focused on goals that are meaningful, gratifying, and consistent with your overall life purpose.

Identifying your core values
Identifying your basic beliefs is an essential step toward matching your financial objectives with your principles. Consider what is most important to you in several facets of life, such as family, relationships, jobs, personal growth, health, community, and spirituality. Consider the following questions to identify your basic values:

1. What gives you the most pleasure and contentment in life?
2. What values or beliefs do you hold dear?
3. What hobbies or endeavors motivate and inspire you?
4. What kind of legacy would you like to leave behind?
5. What values do you want your life to represent?

Exploring these issues and reflecting on your experiences can help you develop clarity on your basic beliefs, which you can then use as a compass to guide your financial decisions and goals.

Aligning Financial Goals and Values
Once you've determined your basic beliefs, the next step is to match your financial objectives with them. Consider how each objective adds to or represents your values and priorities, and ensure that they are in line with what is most important to you. Here's how you can link shared financial objectives with basic values:

1. Family and Relationship: If family and connections are important to you, financial objectives may include saving for family trips, paying for children's education, or helping elderly parents.

2. Personal Growth and Development: If you value personal growth and development, your financial objectives may include investing in education, training, or enrichment activities to improve your skills and knowledge.

3. Health & Wellness: If health and wellness are key objectives, your financial goals may include investing in healthcare, exercise, nutrition, and other wellness-related costs to improve your physical and emotional well-being.

4. Community and Social Impact: If community and social impact are important to you, your financial objectives might include charity giving, volunteering, or supporting causes and organizations that share your beliefs.

5. Financial stability and independence: If financial stability and independence are important, financial objectives may include creating an emergency fund, paying off debt, preparing for retirement, or attaining financial independence.

Aligning your financial objectives with your beliefs gives your quest for financial independence purpose and meaning, making it more gratifying and rewarding.

Advantages of Value-Based Goal Setting
Aligning your financial objectives with your beliefs has various advantages.

1. Boosted motivation and engagement: When your objectives align with your values, you are more inspired and engaged in achieving them, resulting in greater dedication and perseverance in the face of adversity.

2. Increased Satisfaction and Fulfillment: Achieving objectives that are consistent with your beliefs give you a feeling of accomplishment and fulfillment because they represent what is most important to you and enhance your general well-being and health.

3. Enhanced Decision-Making: Values-based goal formulation acts as a guidepost for decision-making, allowing you to prioritize activities and allocate resources to your fundamental values and long-term vision.

4. Lower stress and conflict: When your financial objectives are in line with your values, you have less internal conflict and stress since your actions are consistent with your views and ideals.

Conclusion

Aligning your financial objectives with your beliefs is an effective method for developing a meaningful and purposeful financial strategy. By establishing your essential beliefs and ensuring that your objectives mirror those values, you may seek financial independence with clarity, purpose, and honesty. Stay loyal to what is most important to you, and allow your values to lead you toward financial success and joy.

Chapter 4: Budgeting and Cash Flow Management

4.1 Setting Up a Personal Budget

Budgeting is the foundation of financial management, giving a road map for allocating revenue, limiting spending, and meeting financial objectives. Chapter 4 delves into the importance of creating a personal budget, step-by-step budget design instructions, and strategies for effectively managing your financial flow.

Understanding the Importance of Budgeting
Budgeting is the process of planning and monitoring your income and spending to ensure that you're staying within your means and moving toward your financial goals. It allows you to get insight into your financial status, find areas for growth, and make sound choices about how to best utilize your resources.

The benefits of budgeting:
1. Financial Awareness: Budgeting helps you understand where your money comes from and where it goes, giving you insight into your spending patterns and financial goals.

2. Expense Control: By monitoring your expenditures and sticking to a budget, you may discover areas where you're overpaying and make changes to save costs and waste.

3. Goal Achievement: Budgeting allows you to manage resources toward your financial objectives, such as emergency savings, debt repayment, or long-term investments.

4. Debt Reduction: A well-planned budget may help you prioritize debt payments and expedite your journey to debt freedom.

5. Financial Stability: Budgeting provides financial security and peace of mind by ensuring that you have a strategy in place to successfully manage your money and weather unforeseen bills or crises.

Steps for Creating a Personal Budget:
1. Collect financial information: Begin by collecting information about your income, including salaries, wages, bonuses, commissions, and any other types of compensation. Gather paperwork for your costs, such as bills, receipts, statements, and records of discretionary spending.

2. Calculate Your Revenue: Add together all of your revenue sources to get your total monthly earnings. If your income fluctuates from month to month, take an average of your previous earnings to estimate your monthly income.

3. List your costs: Make a detailed list of your costs, classifying them as fixed (e.g., rent/mortgage, utilities, insurance) and variable (e.g., groceries, transportation, entertainment). Don't forget to mention recurring costs, such as yearly subscriptions and irregular payments.

4. Track Your Spending: For a month or two, track your spending patterns to acquire insight into your regular expenditures and find areas where you could be overpaying or underestimating prices.

5. Set financial goals: Determine your short-term and long-term financial objectives, such as creating an emergency fund, paying off debt, saving for a significant purchase, or investing for retirement. Each month, use your budget to allocate dollars to these targets.

6. Make a Budget Template: Using a spreadsheet, budgeting tool, or pen and paper, build a budget template outlining your income, spending, and savings objectives. Based on your financial priorities and available resources, budget money for each spending area.

7. Adjust and review regularly. Maintain flexibility with your budget and be willing to make changes as required. Review your budget regularly to assess your progress, detect deviations from your plan, and make modifications as needed.

Tips for Effective Budgeting

1. Be realistic: Make realistic budget projections and avoid overestimating income or underestimating costs. Allow for unforeseen expenses and income variations to ensure that your budget is sustainable.

2. Prioritize Essentials: Prioritize necessities like housing, utilities, food, and transportation before allocating cash to discretionary expenditure areas.

3. Use envelopes or categories: Think about utilizing the envelope system or budgeting categories to devote cash to specified expenditures and prevent overpaying in discretionary areas.

4. Automate Savings: Make automated transfers or deductions to savings or investing accounts to guarantee that you are constantly saving for your financial objectives.

5. Monitor Your Progress: Regularly review your budget and monitor your progress toward your financial objectives. Celebrate milestones and victories along the way to keep yourself motivated and involved in the budgeting process.

Conclusion

Making a personal budget is an important step toward financial stability, controlling cash flow, and attaining your financial objectives. By adhering to these rules and incorporating budgeting best practices into your daily routine, you can regain control of your money, make educated decisions, and strive for a better financial future. Stay consistent, and attentive, and watch how your budget helps you reach your goals.

4.2 Tracking Expenses

Tracking your costs is a critical component of successful budgeting and cash flow management. In Chapter 4, we discuss the importance of recording spending, different tracking techniques, and how to use this information to improve your financial situation.

The Importance of Expense Tracking

Expense monitoring involves documenting and classifying every transaction you make, from major purchases to small everyday costs. While it may seem monotonous, cost monitoring is an effective tool for understanding your spending patterns, finding areas for improvement, and making sound financial choices.

The Benefits of Expense Tracking:
1. Financial Awareness: By keeping track of your expenses, you can see exactly where your money is going. It helps you see trends in your spending habits and understand your financial priorities.

2. Budget Alignment: By comparing your actual costs to your planned numbers, you may find anomalies and make changes to ensure that your spending is consistent with your financial objectives.

3. Identifying Problem Areas: Expense monitoring allows you to identify areas where you may be overspending or where costs are greater than expected. This knowledge helps you take remedial action and modify your budget or spending patterns.

4. Goal Progress: Tracking your spending helps you track your progress toward financial objectives. It helps you better deploy resources and prioritize expenditures in areas that contribute to your goals.

5. Financial Accountability: Expense monitoring keeps you responsible for your spending habits. It promotes responsible spending and discourages impulsive purchases by increasing your awareness of the consequences of your actions.

How to track expenses:
1. Manual Tracking: One of the most basic methods to manage spending is to manually enter each transaction in a notepad, spreadsheet, or expense tracking tool. This approach entails noting the date, amount, and category of each cost as you make purchases.

2. Receiver Tracking: Keep all receipts from your purchases and classify them appropriately. At the end of each day or week, enter the information into a budgeting program or spreadsheet to keep track of your expenses.

3. Bank accounts: Regularly, review your bank and credit card accounts to identify and classify your spending. Many banks include online tools that automatically classify transactions, making it easy to monitor your expenditure.

4. Expenditure Tracking Applications: A variety of expenditure tracking applications are available to automate the cost monitoring process. These applications integrate with your bank accounts and credit cards, classify transactions, and give information about your spending patterns.

5. Envelope System: The envelope system involves allocating funds to various spending categories and storing them in labeled envelopes. As you make purchases, subtract the amount from the appropriate envelope to create a visual picture of your expenditure.

Suggestions for Effective Expense Tracking:
1. Be consistent: Make it a habit to document every transaction quickly. Consistency is essential for gaining an accurate picture of your spending patterns.

2. Use Categories: Sort your spending into categories like housing, transportation, groceries, entertainment, and miscellaneous. This enables you to track where your money is going and discover areas for improvement.

3. Analyze Regularly: Set aside time each week or month to analyze your costs and evaluate your spending habits. Search for patterns, outliers, or places where you can cut down.

4. Adjust as Needed: Use the information gained from your cost monitoring to make changes to your budget and spending patterns. Be open to changing your financial strategy to meet your changing requirements and circumstances.

5. Remain Motivated: Recognize minor triumphs and milestones along the road to keep yourself going. Seeing progress toward your financial objectives may give you motivation to keep track of your spending and stay within your budget.

Conclusion
Tracking your spending is essential for good budgeting and cash flow management. You can take charge of your money and strive toward a more secure financial future by learning about your spending patterns, finding areas for improvement, and aligning your costs with your financial objectives. Stay vigilant, observant, and observant as your dedication to spending monitoring pays off in meeting your financial goals.

4.3 Cash Management Strategies

Cash flow management is an essential component of financial stability and success. In this portion of Chapter 4, we will look at numerous ways to properly manage cash flow, ensuring that you have adequate liquidity to meet costs, save for the future, and achieve your financial objectives.

Understanding Cash Flow Management
Cash flow management involves tracking the inflow and outflow of funds in your accounts. It includes tasks like budgeting, cost tracking, income monitoring, and optimizing payment and reception scheduling to provide enough liquidity and financial stability.

The Importance of Cash Flow Management:
1. Guarantees Financial Stability: Effective cash flow management guarantees that you have adequate liquid assets to meet your financial commitments and emergencies, lowering your chances of financial difficulty or bankruptcy.

2. Improves Goal Achievement: By optimizing cash flow, you may more effectively allocate money to savings, investments, and financial goals, speeding progress toward long-term goals like retirement, homeownership, or financial independence.

3. Decreases Debt Dependency: Effective cash flow management decreases the need to borrow and rely on credit to satisfy short-term financial demands, lowering interest costs and debt buildup over time.

4. Provides Flexibility and Security: Having a steady cash flow gives you the ability to weather economic downturns, unforeseen bills, or income interruptions without resorting to harsh measures or financial hardship.

5. Supports company operations: Effective cash flow management is critical for entrepreneurs and small company owners to maintain business operations, control costs, and ensure business continuity and expansion.

Cash-Flow Management Strategies:
1. Create a Cash Flow Statement: Begin by developing a cash flow statement that shows your monthly revenue and spending. This summary gives a picture of your cash inflows and outflows, allowing you to spot surpluses or deficits and make more educated financial choices.

2. Establish an Emergency Fund: Set up an emergency fund to meet unforeseen needs or income fluctuations. Set aside three to six months' worth of living costs in a liquid, easily accessible account, such as a high-yield savings account or money market fund.

3. Prioritize important costs: Determine and prioritize your important costs, such as housing, utilities, food, and insurance. Make sure these expenditures are met first before allocating cash to discretionary spending areas.

4. Monitor and adjust spending: Keep track of your costs and search for ways to cut discretionary spending. Cut down on unnecessary expenditures, identify strategies to reduce recurrent costs, and avoid lifestyle inflation to free up cash flow for savings and investing.

5. Negotiate bills and expenses: Work with service providers, creditors, and vendors to reduce your bills, interest rates, or fees. Consider refinancing debt, moving to lower-cost suppliers, or combining services to save costs and increase cash flow.

6. Optimize Income Sources: Look for ways to supplement your income by working part-time, freelancing, consulting, or passively. Maximize your earning potential by leveraging your talents, knowledge, and assets to generate additional revenue.

7. Use Technology Tools: Automate cash flow monitoring and simplify financial procedures by using technology tools such as budgeting apps, expenditure trackers, and

financial management software. These applications may provide real-time financial data, allowing you to make more educated budgeting and spending choices.

8. Manage Debt Wisely: Create a debt repayment strategy to gradually pay off high-interest debt. Prioritize debts with the highest interest rates or lowest amounts first (the debt snowball or debt avalanche approach) to speed up debt repayment and enhance cash flow over time.

9. Forecast Cash Flow: Plan for future cash flows by developing cash flow forecasts or projections based on predicted revenue and spending. This enables you to prepare for forthcoming commitments, anticipate possible cash gaps, and take proactive steps to reduce financial risk.

10. Review and adjust regularly. Evaluate your cash flow management techniques regularly and make changes as appropriate. Monitor changes in income, spending, and financial goals, and adjust your cash flow strategy accordingly to ensure long-term financial stability and success.

Conclusion

Effective cash flow management is critical for establishing financial stability, reducing debt, and pursuing long-term financial objectives. You may maintain healthy cash flow, create financial resilience, and move toward a more secure financial future by following techniques such as producing a cash flow statement, setting up an emergency fund, prioritizing critical costs, tracking spending, and maximizing revenue sources. Stay proactive, observant, and observant as your dedication to cash flow management results in increased financial independence and peace of mind.

Chapter 5: Debt Management and Elimination

5.1 Understanding Different Types of Debt

Debt is a financial commitment that occurs when you borrow money from a lender or creditor and promise to return it over time, often with interest. In Chapter 5, we will look at the many sorts of debt, their characteristics, and how to manage and eliminate debt successfully.

Types of Debt

1. Consumer debt:

Credit Card Debt: One of the most widespread types of consumer debt is caused by the use of credit cards to make purchases. Credit card debt usually has high-interest rates, making it expensive to carry over time.

Personal Loans: Unsecured loans received from banks, credit unions, or internet lenders for a variety of reasons, including debt consolidation, home upgrades, or unforeseen needs. Personal loans may have fixed or variable interest rates, depending on creditworthiness and payback arrangements.

Payday Loans: These are short-term, high-interest loans that are often utilized by those with bad credit or who need money right away. Payday loans frequently include excessive fees and interest rates, locking consumers in debt cycles.

Installment Loans: Loans have fixed repayment schedules in which borrowers make monthly payments (installments) over a certain period until the loan is entirely repaid. Examples include vehicle loans, school loans, and personal installment loans.

2. Mortgage Debt:

Home Mortgages: Loans used to fund the acquisition of real estate, such as main residences, second houses, or investment properties. Home mortgages are secured by the property itself and usually have lower interest rates than consumer financing.

Home Equity Loans and Lines of Credit: Loans backed by a home's equity enable homeowners to borrow against the property's worth. Home equity loans provide one lump sum payment, while home equity lines of credit (HELOCs) give a revolving line of credit comparable to a credit card.

3. Students' Loans:

Federal Student Loans: Loans provided by the federal government to cover higher education costs such as tuition, fees, books, and living expenses. Federal student loans provide numerous repayment alternatives, such as income-based repayment plans and debt forgiveness programs.

Private Student Loans: Loans taken from private lenders, such as banks or financial organizations, to complement government financial help for educational purposes. Private student loans may have higher interest rates and fewer favorable conditions than government loans.

4. Business debt:

Business Loans: Financing received by enterprises to support operations, growth, or capital projects. Business loans may be secured or unsecured based on the borrower's creditworthiness and collateral.

Business Lines of Credit: Firms can use revolving lines of credit to meet short-term financial requirements such as inventory purchases, payroll, or working capital. Business lines of credit provide flexibility and liquidity to help manage cash flow variations.

5. Other forms of debt:

Auto Loans: Loans for the purchase of vehicles, such as automobiles, trucks, motorbikes, and recreational vehicles. Auto loans may be secured by the vehicle itself and usually have specified payback periods.

Medical Debt: Debt resulting from medical costs such as hospital bills, doctor's fees, prescription prescriptions, and medical treatments. Medical debt may occur abruptly as a result of sickness, an accident, or emergency medical care.

Tax Debt: Amounts due to the government, such as unpaid income taxes, property taxes, or IRS tax obligations. Tax debt may arise from failure to submit taxes, underpayment of taxes, or IRS audits.

Considerations for Debt Management

1. Interest Rates: Different forms of debt have different interest rates, which may greatly affect the overall cost of borrowing. To reduce interest expenditures and hasten debt payback, pay off high-interest debt first.

2. Repayment conditions: Examine the repayment conditions for each loan, including the monthly payment amount, interest rate, and payback time.

Choose repayment plans that are consistent with your financial objectives and cash flow requirements.

3. Secured vs. Unsecured Debt: Determine if your debt is secured by collateral (secured debt) or is unsecured. Secured debt may have lower interest rates, but if payments are not made on time, the asset may be repossessed.

4. The Impact on Credit Score: Keep track of how debt affects your credit score and creditworthiness. Timely payments and appropriate debt management may help boost your credit score over time; however, missed payments or defaults can harm your credit history.

5. Debt-to-income ratio: To determine your debt-to-income ratio, compare your total monthly debt payments to your gross monthly income. A lower debt-to-income ratio means less financial hardship and a better chance of loan approval for future borrowing.

Conclusion

Understanding the many forms of debt is critical to efficient debt management and eradication. You may get control of your debt by reviewing your loan portfolio, prioritizing repayment options, and making educated financial choices. Stay watchful and diligent, and watch as your efforts result in more financial independence and peace of mind.

5.2 Establish a Debt Repayment Plan

Creating a structured debt repayment plan is critical to properly managing and reducing debt. In this portion of Chapter 5, we will look at how to create a customized debt payback plan based on your financial status, objectives, and priorities.

Understanding Debt Repayment

Debt repayment is the methodical return of outstanding debts by a predefined plan or strategy. While it may seem frightening, having a detailed payback plan may help you reclaim control of your money, save interest costs, and eventually achieve debt independence.

Benefits of Debt Repayment Plans:

1. The Clear Path to Debt Freedom: A structured repayment plan lays out a strategy for paying off debt, breaking it down into achievable phases and milestones.

2. Reduced Interest Expenses: By focusing on high-interest debt and making additional payments wherever feasible, you may reduce interest expenses and speed up debt repayment.

3. Improved Financial Health: Paying off debt improves your financial health and stability, lowering financial stress and freeing up resources for other financial objectives and priorities.

4. Enhanced Credit Score: Regular debt repayment and good financial conduct may help you enhance your credit score over time, making it simpler to qualify for future loans and credit on better terms.

Steps to Create a Debt Repayment Plan:

1. List your bills: Begin by making a detailed list of all of your ongoing bills, including the creditor's name, outstanding amount, interest rate, minimum monthly payment, and due date. Organize your bills from smallest to greatest balance (the debt snowball approach) or highest to lowest interest rate (the debt avalanche method).

2. Assess Your Financial Situation: Determine how much money you can set aside each month for debt repayment based on your income, expenditures, and available funds. Consider reducing discretionary spending, boosting income via side hustles or part-time employment, and allocating windfalls or bonuses to debt repayment.

3. Choose a Repayment Approach: Choose a debt repayment approach that is consistent with your financial objectives and preferences. The debt snowball technique prioritizes paying off the smallest debt first, whereas the debt avalanche method focuses on paying off the debt with the greatest interest rate first.

4. Set SMART Goals: Define precise, measurable, attainable, relevant, and time-bound (SMART) debt payback objectives. Determine how much you want to pay off each

month, the date you want to be debt-free, and milestones to help you measure your progress.

5. Negotiate with creditors: Contact your creditors to discuss possibilities for decreasing interest rates, waiving fees, or negotiating settlement terms. Many creditors are prepared to work with you to create a repayment plan that works for your budget and financial situation.

6. Make a Budget: Create a realistic budget that allocates money to debt repayment while also covering necessary spending and savings objectives. Track your expenditures, make adjustments to your budget as required, and maintain discipline in keeping with your financial plan.

7. Allocate Extra Payments: Whenever feasible, use any additional income, such as tax refunds, bonuses, or windfalls, to repay debt. Making extra payments toward principal amounts might help you pay off debt quicker and save on interest.

8. Monitor Your Progress: Review your debt repayment plan regularly and keep track of your progress toward your objectives. Celebrate milestones and victories along the way to keep yourself motivated and involved in the debt repayment process.

Suggestions for Successful Debt Repayment:

1. Stay Focused: Remain focused on your objective of becoming debt-free. Avoid temptation and stick to your debt payback strategy even when confronted with setbacks or problems.

2. Celebrate Small Wins: Recognize each debt paid off and milestone achieved along the road. Recognizing your efforts and triumphs may improve morale and keep you encouraged to continue your debt-free path.

3. Seek Support: If you're dealing with debt repayment, don't be afraid to seek help from friends, family, or support groups. Having a support system may provide encouragement, accountability, and useful counsel during difficult times.

4. Stay Flexible: Be adaptive and flexible during your debt reduction journey. Job loss, medical problems, or big costs are all examples of unforeseen life events that may require changes to your repayment plan. To remain on track toward your objectives, keep flexible and make adjustments as required.

Conclusion

Creating a structured debt repayment plan is critical to properly managing and reducing debt. By taking these actions, you may regain control of your finances, reduce debt stress, and move toward a debt-free future. Stay patient, and persistent, and observe as your efforts result in more financial independence and peace of mind.

5.3 Tips for Accelerating Debt Repayment

Accelerating debt repayment entails using ideas and procedures to pay off debts faster, lowering interest rates, and gaining financial independence sooner. In this portion of Chapter 5, we will look at practical strategies for expediting debt repayment and obtaining your debt-free status.

1. Increase your debt payments.

One of the most efficient techniques to speed up debt repayment is to raise your monthly loan payments. Any excess earnings, such as bonuses, tax refunds, or windfalls, should be used to pay off debt. Making larger payments allows you to pay down the main amount faster, lowering your overall interest charges throughout the loan's life.

2. Use the Debt Snowball or Debt Avalanche Method.

To prioritize your debt payments, consider using the debt snowball or debt avalanche methods. The debt snowball strategy focuses on paying off the lowest loan first, regardless of interest rate, while making minimum payments on the other obligations. Once the lowest debt is paid off, the payment amount is rolled into the next smallest loan, resulting in a snowball effect. In contrast, the debt avalanche strategy entails prioritizing bills with the highest interest rates first while making minimal payments on other obligations. This strategy reduces overall interest expenses over time.

3. Consolidate and refinance high-interest debt.

Investigate the possibility of consolidating or refinancing high-interest debt to lower interest rates and simplify payments. Consolidation combines various debts into a single loan with a reduced interest rate, while refinancing enables you to replace current debt with a new credit on better terms. Look for ways to consolidate or restructure high-interest credit card debt, personal loans, or school loans to save money on interest and speed up debt repayment.

4. Reduce expenses and increase income.

Identify areas where you can cut costs and redirect money to debt reduction. Reduce your discretionary expenditures, such as eating out, entertainment, and luxury products, and put those amounts toward debt repayment. Consider earning extra money via side hustles, part-time jobs, freelancing projects, or selling unneeded stuff. Every dollar saved or earned may be used to accelerate debt repayment and achieve your financial objectives quickly.

5. Implement a cash-only spending policy.

Switch to a cash-only spending approach to avoid incurring new debt while repaying old obligations. To reduce spending and remain within your budget, make purchases using cash or debit cards rather than credit cards. Using cash makes you more aware of your spending patterns and less likely to splurge on unneeded goods. This rigorous strategy might help you remain on track with your debt payback objectives and avoid getting back into debt.

6. Negotiate lower interest rates and fees.

Contact your creditors to negotiate reduced interest rates, fees, or penalty costs on your current loans. Explain your financial condition and show your willingness to repay the amount. Many creditors are ready to negotiate with borrowers to lower interest rates or remove fees, particularly if you have a track record of regular payments or are facing financial difficulties. Lowering your interest rates may drastically cut the overall cost of borrowing and speed up debt repayment.

7. Stay Motivated and Celebrate Milestones.

Keep yourself motivated and focused on your debt repayment objectives by recognizing milestones and accomplishments along the way. Set tiny goals, such as paying off a single loan or achieving a certain percentage of overall debt paid off, and celebrate each accomplishment. Recognize the sacrifices and hard work you've put into paying off your obligations, and use these milestones as inspiration to keep moving forward toward debt freedom.

8. Avoid temptation and maintain discipline.

To avoid sliding back into debt, resist temptation and practice financial discipline. Despite enticing offers or social pressure, resist the impulse to splurge or incur additional debt. Maintain your debt repayment strategy and concentrate on the long-term rewards of obtaining financial independence. Remember that every dollar you save or earn brings you one step closer to being debt-free.

Conclusion

To pay off debt faster, you must be dedicated, disciplined, and strategic. Implementing these suggestions and practices can allow you to pay off your debts faster, save money on interest, and reach financial independence sooner. Stay focused, and determined, and watch as your efforts result in a brighter financial future free of debt.

Crossing The Gap

Chapter 6: Emergency Funding and Risk Management

6.1: The Importance of an Emergency Fund

Few ideas in personal finance are more extensively highlighted yet often disregarded than the emergency fund. An emergency fund serves as a financial safety net, protecting against unexpected bills, income interruptions, and unanticipated occurrences. In this chapter, we will look at the significance of having an emergency fund, its advantages, and how to develop and manage one efficiently.

Understanding the Role of Emergency Funds

Consider the following scenarios: your vehicle abruptly breaks down, your pet needs emergency medical attention, or you are suddenly laid off. In such cases, having an emergency fund may make the difference between financial security and disaster. An emergency fund is a quickly available pool of cash that you may use to meet unforeseen bills or income gaps without incurring high-interest debt, selling assets, or depending on other sources of assistance.

The Importance of Emergency Funds:

1. Financial Security: Having an emergency fund gives you a feeling of security and peace of mind since you know you have a financial buffer to fall back on in times of need. It relieves the tension and worry caused by unexpected costs or income interruptions, enabling you to face problems with confidence.

2. Debt Protection: Having cash reserves on hand allows you to avoid using high-interest credit cards, payday loans, or other types of debt to meet unexpected needs. This helps to avoid debt building and reduces the long-term financial burden of unforeseen occurrences.

3. Preservation of Assets: An emergency fund helps you protect your assets and investments during times of financial crisis. Instead of liquidating assets or selling treasured belongings to earn money, you may use your emergency reserves to pay urgent expenditures while still meeting your long-term financial objectives.

4. Flexibility and Freedom: Having an emergency reserve allows you to make financial decisions with more freedom. It enables you to manage unforeseen expenditures or

capture opportunities without interrupting your financial strategy or endangering your long-term objectives.

5. Mitigation of Financial Risks: Life is unpredictable, and unanticipated occurrences might occur at any time. Whether it's a medical emergency, house repair, or job loss, having an emergency fund helps to manage financial risks and buffers against the effects of unexpected events.

Create an Emergency Fund:

Now that we understand the need for an emergency fund, let's look at some practical techniques for developing one:

1. Set savings goals: Determine how much you should save for an emergency fund depending on your financial condition, spending, and risk tolerance. Financial experts normally suggest saving three to six months' worth of living costs; however, the exact amount may vary based on personal circumstances.

2. Start modest: If you're just starting with your emergency fund, start modest and steadily expand your savings over time. Set attainable benchmarks and celebrate each one met to keep motivated and dedicated to your financial objectives.

3. Automate Savings: Set up automatic transfers from your checking account to a savings account specifically allocated for your emergency fund. Automating your savings allows you to consistently save a percentage of your money without having to actively manage it.

4. Cut costs: Examine your monthly costs to discover areas where you may reduce or eliminate discretionary spending. Redirect your money to your emergency fund to boost its growth. Consider adopting economical habits such as cooking at home, canceling subscriptions, or looking for cheaper alternatives to save costs.

5. Increase Income: Look for ways to supplement your income by working part-time, freelancing, or starting a side venture. Use the additional money to increase your emergency fund savings and achieve your objectives faster.

6. Prioritize Savings: Make emergency savings a top priority in your financial strategy. Treat it as a non-negotiable cost, similar to paying bills or saving for retirement. Prioritizing savings ensures that you continually increase your emergency fund and plan for unforeseen costs.

7. Avoid temptations: resist the urge to spend your emergency money on non-essential costs or impulsive purchases. Keep your emergency funds separate from your regular accounts and use them only for actual situations.

How to Maintain an Emergency Fund:

Building an emergency fund is merely the first step; keeping it up demands consistent attention and discipline. Here are some suggestions for efficiently managing and protecting your emergency savings:

1. Regularly Review costs: Review your costs and change your budget as required to ensure that your emergency fund is sufficiently filled. Adjust your savings goals to reflect any changes in your financial situation, such as changes in income or spending.

2. Refill After Withdrawals: If you need to draw from your emergency fund to pay unforeseen expenditures, make it a point to refill the money as quickly as possible. Continue making monthly payments to your emergency fund until it reaches the goal amount again.

3. Monitor Interest Rates: Keep track of the interest rates given by banks and financial institutions for savings or money market accounts. To optimize your savings over time, consider transferring your emergency fund to accounts with higher returns or better conditions.

4. Examine savings objectives: As your financial circumstances change, examine and revise your emergency savings objectives as necessary. To achieve appropriate financial security, you may need to revise your savings objectives due to changes in income, spending, family size, or financial goals.

5. Use windfalls. Wisely: Use unexpected windfalls like tax returns, bonuses, or inheritances to build an emergency fund or expedite debt repayment. Avoid the temptation to overspend on non-essential things and instead focus on establishing financial stability for the future.

Conclusion:

In conclusion, an emergency fund is essential for financial stability and resilience. Setting up and maintaining an emergency fund protects you against unexpected bills, income interruptions, and financial crises. Begin growing your emergency fund now, and enjoy the peace of mind that comes with knowing you're ready for anything life throws at you.

6.2 Establishing and Maintaining Your Emergency Fund

Few personal financial ideas are more well-accepted than the need for an emergency fund. An emergency fund serves as a financial safety net, protecting against unexpected bills, income interruptions, and unanticipated occurrences. In this part, we'll go over the most important components of creating and managing an emergency fund to guarantee financial stability and resilience.

Building Your Emergency Fund

Creating an emergency fund involves careful preparation, disciplined saving habits, and a dedication to financial readiness. Here are crucial measures to consider while setting up your emergency fund:

1. Set realistic goals: Start by establishing how much you need to save for an emergency fund. Financial advisers often suggest saving three to six months' worth of living costs, while the exact amount varies depending on individual variables such as income stability, family size, and job security.

2. Start small: If you're new to saving or have limited resources, don't give up. Begin small and progressively build your savings over time. Setting up a tiny amount each week or month might add up over time and help you build an emergency fund.

3. Automate Savings: Set up automatic transfers from your checking account to a savings account specifically designated for your emergency fund. Automating your savings promotes consistency and minimizes the temptation to spend money on unnecessary purchases.

4. Cut costs: Examine your monthly costs to discover areas where you may reduce or eliminate discretionary spending. Redirect your money to your emergency fund to boost its growth. Consider reducing spending on things like eating out, entertainment, subscriptions, and impulsive purchases.

5. Increase Income: Look for ways to supplement your income by working part-time, freelancing, or starting a side business. Use the additional money to increase your emergency fund savings and achieve your objectives faster. Look for methods to commercialize your skills, interests, or abilities to earn extra money.

6. Prioritize Savings: Make saving for your emergency fund a non-negotiable budget item. Prioritize it alongside other necessary costs such as rent, electricity, and debt repayment. Consistently saving a percentage of your salary guarantees that you make continuous progress toward your emergency fund objectives.

7. Use Windfalls Wisely: Take advantage of unexpected windfalls like tax returns, bonuses, or financial gifts to boost your emergency fund reserves. Instead of spending

on unnecessary goods, use windfall revenues to improve your financial stability and peace of mind.

8. Remain focused and disciplined. Creating an emergency fund takes discipline and perseverance. Stay focused on your savings objectives and avoid using your emergency fund for non-essential purchases. Keep your eyes on the target and take a long-term approach to financial readiness.

Maintain Your Emergency Fund

Once you've built your emergency fund, you must successfully manage it to guarantee long-term financial stability. Here are some ways to manage and preserve your emergency savings:

1. Regularly examine costs: To ensure that your emergency fund is sufficiently funded, examine your costs and budget regularly. Take into account any changes in your financial situation, such as income fluctuations, costs, or life events, and revise your savings targets accordingly.

2. Refill After Withdrawals: If you need to draw from your emergency fund to pay unforeseen expenditures, make it a point to refill the money as quickly as possible. Continue making monthly payments to your emergency fund until it reaches the goal amount again.

3. Monitor Interest Rates: Keep track of the interest rates offered by banks or financial institutions for savings or money market accounts. To optimize your savings over time, consider transferring your emergency fund to accounts with higher returns or better conditions.

4. Examine savings objectives: As your financial circumstances change, examine and revise your emergency savings objectives as necessary. To achieve appropriate financial security, you may need to revise your savings objectives due to changes in income, spending, family size, or financial goals.

5. Stay Prepared for Emergencies: Be alert and ready for unforeseen costs or income fluctuations. While it is hard to anticipate every financial crisis, having an emergency fund gives you peace of mind and confidence that you are prepared to face whatever life throws at you.

6. Avoid temptations: Resist the urge to spend your emergency money on non-essential costs or impulsive purchases. Keep your emergency funds separate from your regular accounts, and use them only for actual situations.

Conclusion

Building and maintaining an emergency fund is essential for financial stability and resilience. You can build a strong financial safety net by using these tactics and ideas to defend against unexpected bills and income interruptions. Start saving for an emergency fund now and enjoy the peace of mind that comes with knowing you're ready for anything life throws at you.

6.3 Insurance Planning for Financial Security

Insurance is essential for reducing financial risks and protecting against unanticipated occurrences that might affect your financial security. In this part, we'll look at the significance of insurance planning, various forms of insurance coverage, and ways to guarantee complete financial security.

Understanding insurance planning

Insurance planning is the process of assessing your financial risks and devising solutions to shift those risks to an insurance company in exchange for premium payments. By purchasing insurance, you protect yourself and your loved ones against potential financial losses caused by accidents, sickness, property damage, liability claims, or other unforeseen circumstances.

Various types of insurance coverage

1. Health Insurance: Health insurance covers medical expenditures related to disease, injury, or preventative treatment. It helps reduce the expense of hospitalization, doctor visits, prescriptions, and other healthcare services. Health insurance may be acquired via employer-sponsored plans, government programs like Medicaid or Medicare, or commercial insurance companies.

2. Life Insurance: Life insurance offers financial security for your beneficiaries in the event of your death. It distributes lump sum or recurring payments to chosen beneficiaries upon your death, assisting in the replacement of lost income, the payment of funeral costs, the settlement of debts, or the provision of financial assistance for dependents. There are many types of life insurance plans available, including term life, whole life, universal life, and variable life.

3. Disability Insurance: Disability insurance provides income replacement if you are unable to work due to sickness or accident. It pays out a percentage of your pre-disability income to help you manage living costs, medical bills, and other financial responsibilities while you are disabled. Disability insurance is available via employer-sponsored plans, commercial insurers, and government programs such as Social Security Disability Insurance (SSDI).

4. Auto Insurance: In the event of an accident, auto insurance provides coverage for vehicle damage and liability. It often includes collision coverage, which pays for car

repairs or replacements, as well as liability coverage, which protects people from personal harm and property damage. Optional coverages available with auto insurance include comprehensive coverage, uninsured or underinsured motorist coverage, and personal injury protection (PIP).

5. Homeowners/Renters Insurance: Homeowners insurance protects your house and personal possessions against damage or loss caused by hazards such as fire, theft, vandalism, or natural catastrophe. It covers housing replacement, personal property, liability protection, and extra living costs if your home becomes uninhabitable. Renters insurance provides comparable coverage to renters who rent a residence, covering their items and providing liability coverage.

6. Umbrella Insurance: Umbrella insurance extends liability protection beyond the scope of your basic insurance coverage. It provides an additional layer of protection against catastrophic catastrophes or litigation that exceed the limits of your car, home, or renter's insurance. Umbrella insurance is particularly beneficial to high-net-worth individuals or those with large assets to protect.

Insurance Planning Strategies

1. Assess Your Insurance Needs: Consider your financial status, lifestyle, and risk tolerance when determining the kinds and levels of insurance coverage you need. Consider income, assets, responsibilities, dependents, health condition, and lifestyle when tailoring your insurance portfolio to your unique requirements.

2. Shop Around for Coverage: Compare quotes from several insurance companies to discover the best coverage choices at affordable prices. When purchasing an insurance policy, consider coverage limitations, deductibles, premiums, policy features, and customer service.

3. Review and Update Coverage regularly: Make sure your insurance coverage is up-to-date and meets your changing requirements and circumstances. Life events such as marriage, divorce, childbirth, a house purchase, or a professional shift may require changes to your insurance plans.

4. Bundle Policies for Savings: To qualify for multi-policy savings, bundle several insurance policies from the same provider, such as vehicle and home insurance. Bundling can result in significant savings on premiums while also simplifying insurance administration.

5. Maximize Discounts and Savings: Take advantage of any discounts and savings possibilities provided by insurance companies. Discounts may be provided for characteristics like safe driving records, home security systems, multi-car plans, loyalty, and longevity with the insurance company.

6. When choosing insurance plans, consider the trade-off between deductibles and coverage limitations. Higher deductibles may decrease your rates, but they may mean paying more out of pocket in the case of a claim. Similarly, make sure that your coverage levels are appropriate to protect your assets and liabilities from any dangers.

Conclusion

Insurance planning is an important part of comprehensive financial planning since it protects you and gives you peace of mind in the face of unexpected events. Understanding your insurance requirements, choosing suitable coverage, and applying risk management measures can help you protect your financial well-being and prepare for the unexpected. Take proactive efforts to frequently assess your insurance portfolio, shop around for competitive prices, and verify that your coverage is enough to suit your changing requirements. With effective insurance planning, you can lay a firm foundation for financial stability and resilience, shielding yourself and your loved ones from unexpected risks and obstacles.

Chapter 7: An Introduction to Investing

7.1 Investment Fundamentals and Principles

Investing is a key component of wealth creation and financial success. It entails putting your money to work with the hope of earning returns over time. In this part, we will look at the foundations of investing, such as essential concepts, techniques, and things to think about before starting your investment journey.

Understanding Investment Basics

At its core, investing is the act of allocating resources, such as money or assets, to create income or capital growth. Investors seek to expand their wealth over time by acquiring assets with the potential to appreciate, such as stocks, bonds, real estate, and mutual funds.

Key Investment Principles:

1. Risk and Return: The link between risk and return is a basic investment idea. Generally, investments with larger potential returns have a higher amount of risk. Investors must examine their risk tolerance and investing objectives to strike an optimal risk-reward balance that is consistent with their financial goals.

2. Diversification: Diversification is a risk management approach in which assets are distributed among many asset classes, sectors, geographic locations, and investment vehicles. Diversifying their portfolio allows investors to limit the influence of individual asset performance on total investment returns while also minimizing exposure to particular dangers.

3. Time Horizon: The time horizon is the amount of time an investor intends to keep an investment before having to access cash. Investors with longer time horizons are better able to accept short-term volatility in investment returns and may be more motivated to invest in assets with more growth potential, such as equities.

4. Asset Allocation: Asset allocation is the strategic distribution of investments across several asset classes, such as stocks, bonds, and cash equivalents, depending on an investor's risk tolerance, investment goals, and time horizon. Asset allocation is key to influencing portfolio performance and risk exposure.

5. Costs and Fees: Expense ratios, management fees, and brokerage charges may all have a major influence on long-term investment outcomes. Investors should be aware of their investment costs and aim to reduce them by choosing low-cost investment solutions and avoiding superfluous fees.

Investment Strategies for Beginners:

1. Set Specific Investment Goals: Determine your investment objectives, such as saving for retirement, covering college expenditures, purchasing a property, or attaining financial independence. Setting specific goals helps drive your financial choices and provides a framework for developing your portfolio.

2. Assess Your Risk Tolerance: Determine your risk tolerance by taking into account your investing time horizon, financial condition, investment knowledge, and degree of comfort with market volatility. Understanding your risk tolerance allows you to choose an asset allocation and investing plan that is suitable for your needs and goals.

3. Educate yourself: invest time in learning about various investing possibilities, tactics, and market trends. Reading books, articles, and trustworthy financial periodicals; attending investing seminars or workshops; and seeking advice from financial specialists may all help you improve your investment knowledge and decision-making.

4. Begin with a varied portfolio: Create a varied investment portfolio made up of a variety of asset types, including stocks, bonds, and cash equivalents. Consider investing in low-cost index funds or exchange-traded funds (ETFs) to get broad market exposure and immediate diversification across several sectors and businesses.

5. Remain disciplined and patient. Investing is a long-term undertaking that demands discipline, patience, and a determination to stay the course despite market changes and economic cycles. Avoid making emotional decisions or reacting impulsively to short-term market changes. Maintain your investing strategy and keep focused on your long-term financial objectives.

Conclusion

Investing is an effective instrument for increasing wealth, meeting financial objectives, and safeguarding your financial future. Understanding the basic concepts of investing, defining clear objectives, measuring your risk tolerance, and developing a diverse investment portfolio will help you lay the groundwork for long-term financial prosperity. Take proactive measures to educate yourself on investing possibilities and methods, seek advice from reputable financial advisors, and maintain a disciplined investment attitude. With careful preparation, sound decision-making, and a long-term mindset, you may use investing to increase your wealth and attain financial independence.

7.2: Understanding Risk and Return

In the realm of investing, risk and return are key ideas that every investor must comprehend. These two criteria are closely intertwined, and finding the correct balance is critical for creating a successful investing portfolio. In this section, we will examine the relationship between risk and return, different types of investment hazards, and risk management techniques that maximize returns.

Risk and Return: An Investment Trade-Off

The risk-reward connection is a key investment concept. In general, investments with larger potential returns are associated with higher levels of risk, while investments with reduced risk tend to have lower potential returns. The trade-off between risk and reward is an important issue for investors when making investment choices.

Types of investment risk:

1. Market Risk: Market risk, also known as systematic risk or volatility risk, refers to the danger of investment losses caused by variations in general market conditions. Economic circumstances, interest rates, geopolitical events, and market sentiment all have the potential to influence asset values and cause market volatility. Market risk impacts all assets to some extent and cannot be mitigated via diversification.

2. Interest Rate Risk: Changes in interest rates may impact the value of fixed-income products like bonds. Bond prices typically decrease when interest rates rise and vice versa. Investors are at greater risk when investing in long-term bonds since they are more susceptible to changes in interest rates than short-term bonds.

3. Credit Risk: Credit risk, also known as default risk, is the risk of investment losses resulting from a borrower's failure to meet its financial commitments. Credit risk exists in corporate bonds, municipal bonds, and other fixed-income assets issued by entities of different creditworthiness. Larger-yielding bonds have a greater credit risk, although investment-grade bonds are regarded as less hazardous.

4. Inflation Risk: Inflation risk, also known as purchasing power risk, is the possibility that inflation may reduce the actual value of investment returns over time. Inflation reduces money's buying power, lowering the real value of investment returns. Investments that fail to exceed inflation may result in a loss of buying power in the long run.

5. Liquidity Risk: Liquidity risk is the danger of being unable to acquire or sell an investment promptly and at a reasonable price. Illiquid assets, such as real estate, private equity, or some alternative investments, may be difficult to sell or liquidate at short notice, exposing investors to liquidity risk. When selling an investment, illiquidity might cause delays, increased transaction expenses, or a disadvantageous price.

Strategies for Risk Management and Return Optimization:

1. Diversification: Diversification is a risk management approach in which assets are distributed among many asset classes, sectors, geographic locations, and investment vehicles. Diversifying their portfolios allows investors to limit the influence of individual asset performance on total investment returns while also minimizing exposure to specific risks.

2. Asset Allocation: Asset allocation is the strategic distribution of investments across several asset classes, such as stocks, bonds, and cash equivalents, depending on an investor's risk tolerance, investment goals, and time horizon. Asset allocation is key to influencing portfolio performance and risk exposure.

3. Risk Assessment and Monitoring: Regularly review and monitor your investment portfolio to detect possible hazards and alter your investment plan as needed. Stay current on market conditions, economic trends, and geopolitical events that may affect your assets. Rebalance your portfolio on a regular basis to keep the asset allocation and risk profile you choose.

4. Risk Management Techniques: Use risk management tools like stop-loss orders, hedging methods, or portfolio insurance to mitigate downside risk and reduce possible losses. Consider employing options, futures, or other derivative products to protect against negative market movements or particular risks.

5. Stress Testing and Scenario Analysis: To determine how severe market circumstances or extreme occurrences may affect your investment portfolio, run stress tests and scenario analyses. Identify weaknesses and develop contingency plans to reduce risk and protect money in difficult market conditions.

6. Investment Horizon and Goals: Match your investment horizon and objectives to your risk tolerance and investing approach. When assessing your risk exposure and asset allocation, keep in mind your investment time horizon, liquidity requirements, financial goals, and tolerance for short-term volatility.

Conclusion

Understanding the link between risk and return is critical for making sound investing choices and establishing a profitable portfolio. Investors may improve their investment results while limiting possible losses by identifying different kinds of investment hazards, employing risk management measures, and striking the correct balance between risk and return. To succeed in the fast-paced world of investing, take a proactive approach to risk management, stick to your investment plan, and stay focused on your long-term financial objectives.

Crossing The Gap

Chapter 8: Create an Investment Portfolio

8.1 Asset Allocation Strategy

Building a well-balanced investment portfolio is critical for meeting long-term financial objectives while properly managing risk. Asset allocation is the planned distribution of assets across various asset classes that determines portfolio performance and risk exposure. In this part, we will look at several asset allocation techniques, their advantages, and concerns while building a diversified investment portfolio.

The Importance of Asset Allocation:

Asset allocation is a critical predictor of investing performance, accounting for the vast majority of portfolio returns and risk. According to studies, asset allocation has a greater impact on portfolio performance than individual stock selection or market timing. Diversifying assets across asset classes allows investors to maximize returns while reducing risk and volatility.

Key Asset Class:

1. Stocks: Stocks represent ownership holdings in publicly listed corporations that have the potential for long-term capital growth and dividend income. Stocks are recognized for their greater returns, but they also carry more volatility and risk than other asset groups.

2. Bonds: Bonds are debt instruments issued by governments, municipalities, businesses, or other organizations to generate funds. Bonds provide predictable income streams in the form of interest payments and have lower risk than equities, making them an important component of a diversified portfolio.

3. Cash Equivalents: Cash equivalents, such as money market funds, certificates of deposit (CDs), or Treasury bills, provide stability and liquidity but often yield lower returns than equities and bonds. Cash equivalents act as a haven during market downturns and may offer liquidity for short-term financial needs.

4. Real Estate: Real estate investments include the purchase, ownership, and management of physical assets such as residential residences, commercial structures,

or rental properties. Real estate provides opportunities for rental income, capital gain, and portfolio diversity.

Asset Allocation Strategies:

1. Strategic Asset Allocation: Strategic asset allocation entails determining a target allocation to various asset classes based on long-term investment goals, risk tolerance, and time horizons. The asset allocation remains largely consistent over time, with occasional rebalancing to ensure the target allocation.

2. "Tactical Asset Allocation" Tactical asset allocation is the process of making short-term changes to portfolio allocations in response to market situations, economic trends, or valuation measures. Tactical asset allocation techniques aim to capitalize on short-term opportunities or avoid potential hazards by deviating from strategic asset allocation guidelines.

3. Dynamic Asset Allocation: Dynamic asset allocation incorporates elements of strategic and tactical allocation methodologies, providing flexibility in revising portfolio allocations in response to changing market circumstances or economic outlooks. Dynamic allocation techniques use quantitative models, market data, or qualitative judgments to make investment choices.

4. Risk-Based Asset Allocation: Risk-based asset allocation aims to manage portfolio risk by distributing assets based on risk variables, including volatility, correlation, and downside protection. Risk-based allocation techniques aim to attain a certain degree of risk exposure while maximizing returns within the portfolio's risk limits.

5. Factor-Based Asset Allocation: Factor-based asset allocation considers value, growth, size, momentum, and quality when making investing decisions. Factor-based strategies seek to identify distinct risk premia or market anomalies connected with certain investing characteristics.

Considerations for Asset Allocation

1. Investing Objectives: Align asset allocation with your investing goals, whether they be for capital appreciation, income creation, wealth preservation, or risk management. When deciding on an asset allocation plan, keep your time horizon, liquidity requirements, and financial objectives in mind.

2. Risk Tolerance: Consider your risk tolerance and comfort level with market volatility when deciding on asset classes and portfolio allocations. Conservative investors may choose a more balanced allocation with a larger weighting in fixed income, while aggressive investors may prefer a more growth-oriented allocation with a higher weight in stocks.

3. Diversification: Spread risk and minimize portfolio volatility by investing in a variety of asset classes, industries, geographic locations, and investment strategies.

Diversification reduces the influence of individual asset performance on total portfolio returns while increasing risk-adjusted returns over time.

4. Rebalancing: Review and rebalance your portfolio regularly to ensure that your goal asset allocation and risk profile remain unchanged. Rebalancing entails selling appreciated assets and purchasing underperforming assets to restore the appropriate allocation. Rebalancing ensures that your portfolio stays in line with your investing goals and risk tolerance.

5. Expenses and Taxes: When developing an asset allocation plan, keep in mind the expenses and tax implications of various asset classes and investment vehicles. Reduce investing expenses by choosing low-cost funds or ETFs, and maximize tax efficiency by using tax-advantaged accounts or tax-loss harvesting procedures.

Conclusion:

Asset allocation is a vital component of creating a successful investment portfolio that meets long-term financial objectives while efficiently managing risk. You may maximize returns and confidently handle market volatility by diversifying assets across asset classes, employing a disciplined asset allocation strategy, and rebalancing your portfolio regularly. Consider your investing goals, risk tolerance, and time horizon when developing your asset allocation plan, and seek advice from financial specialists or investment advisers to adapt your portfolio to your unique requirements and preferences. With careful planning and intelligent asset allocation, you may create a robust investment portfolio that can endure market changes and contribute to long-term financial success.

8.2 Diversification Techniques

Diversification is a basic idea of investment portfolio creation that seeks to reduce risk by distributing assets across asset classes, sectors, and geographic locations. Diversifying your portfolio can reduce the influence of individual asset performance on total portfolio returns while increasing risk-adjusted returns over time. In this part, we'll look at numerous diversification approaches and strategies for creating a highly diversified investing portfolio.

1. Asset class diversification:

Asset class diversification entails spreading investments over many asset classes, including equities, bonds, cash equivalents, and real estate. Each asset class has its risk-return profile and responds differently to different market situations.

Diversifying across asset classes allows investors to limit risk while capturing gains from various sources.

Key Considerations:
Determine the best asset allocation based on your investing goals, risk tolerance, and time horizon.
Divide assets across stocks, bonds, and cash equivalents to create a balanced portfolio that offers growth potential, income, and stability.
Consider diversifying your portfolio with alternative assets such as real estate, commodities, or asset classes to improve risk-adjusted returns.

2. Geographic diversity:
Geographic diversification entails investing in securities or assets from several geographical areas and nations. Investing abroad allows investors to decrease their exposure to country-specific risks, currency changes, and geopolitical events. Geographic diversity also helps investors take advantage of the growth potential of developing nations while avoiding concentrated dangers in local markets.

Key Considerations:
To achieve geographic diversity, allocate assets among established, developing, and frontier regions.
When deciding on overseas investments, consider economic growth potential, political stability, the regulatory environment, and currency risk.
Diversify your portfolio geographically by investing in global stock funds, international ETFs, or regional mutual funds.

3. Sector Diversification:
Sector diversification is the process of investing in securities or assets from a variety of economic sectors or businesses. Each industry has its own set of performance drivers, which may alter depending on the economic circumstances. Diversifying across sectors allows investors to limit exposure to sector-specific risks while positioning their portfolios to benefit from opportunities in many industries.

Key Considerations:
To diversify, allocate assets among sectors such as technology, healthcare, consumer discretionary, financials, industrials, and utilities.
Consider sector rotation strategies that use cyclical patterns, economic cycles, or sector-specific triggers to boost portfolio returns.
Regularly monitor sector exposures and rebalance your portfolio to preserve diversity and modify sector weights in response to changing market circumstances.

4. Investment Style Diversification:

Investment style diversification entails purchasing securities or assets with various investment styles, such as growth, value, or income-oriented strategies. Each investing style has unique features and performance factors, which, when combined in a portfolio, may provide diversification advantages. Diversifying investment types allows investors to mitigate style-specific risks while capturing profits from various market scenarios.

Key Considerations:

Divide investments among several investing strategies, such as growth stocks, value stocks, dividend-paying stocks, and income-generating assets.

Consider combining several investment types in your portfolio to create a balanced strategy that includes growth potential, value-oriented options, and income-generating strategies.

Monitor style exposures and modify portfolio allocations in response to changes in market circumstances, investor sentiment, and valuation indicators.

5. Individual Security Diversification:

Individual security diversification entails distributing assets over a diverse selection of individual securities within each asset class or industry. Investors may lower the idiosyncratic risk associated with certain firms or issuers by maintaining a diverse portfolio of individual securities, as well as lessen the effect of unfavorable events on portfolio performance.

Key Considerations:

To reduce risk and increase portfolio resilience, diversify your portfolio by including individual stocks, bonds, and real estate assets.

When picking individual shares for your portfolio, consider firm size, industry exposure, financial health, and value.

Use mutual funds, exchange-traded funds, or index funds as core portfolio holdings to provide wide diversification over hundreds or thousands of distinct stocks in a single investment vehicle.

Conclusion:

Diversification is a significant risk management strategy that may assist investors in developing robust investment portfolios and achieving long-term financial objectives. Diversifying across asset classes, geographic areas, sectors, investing styles, and individual securities allows investors to decrease risk, increase risk-adjusted returns, and confidently handle market turbulence. Implementing diversification strategies takes careful planning, focused execution, and continual monitoring to ensure that your portfolio is well-diversified by your investment goals and risk tolerance. A diverse investment portfolio may help you attain better stability, resilience, and success in the ever-changing world of finance.

8.3 Investment Vehicles and Option

Creating an investment portfolio entail choosing suitable investment vehicles and alternatives that are consistent with your financial objectives, risk tolerance, and investing strategy. Investment vehicles provide the foundation of your portfolio, giving exposure to a variety of asset classes, sectors, and investing techniques. In this section, we will look at the many investment vehicles and alternatives available to investors, as well as the features and factors to consider when integrating them into your portfolio.

1. Stocks:

Stocks represent ownership holdings in publicly listed corporations that have the potential for long-term capital growth and dividend income. Stocks are classified into distinct classes depending on their size, growth potential, and value criteria. Investors might choose a variety of stocks, including common stock, preferred stock, growth stocks, value stocks, and dividend-paying stocks.

Considerations:

When picking individual stocks for your portfolio, consider the company's fundamentals, financial performance, and future growth potential.

Diversify among sectors, industries, and market capitalizations to reduce single-stock risk and capitalize on opportunities across the equities market.

Monitor stock prices, earnings growth, and market trends to make sound investment choices and modify portfolio allocations as appropriate.

2. Bonds:

Bonds are debt instruments issued by governments, municipalities, businesses, and other organizations to generate funds. Bonds provide consistent income streams in the form of interest payments and carry less risk than equities. Bonds are classified according to issuer type, maturity date, credit rating, and coupon payment structure. Common bond types include Treasury bonds, corporate bonds, municipal bonds, and high-yield bonds.

Considerations:

When deciding which bonds to include in your portfolio, consider credit quality, duration, yield, and interest rate sensitivity.

Diversify among bond issuers, sectors, and maturities to mitigate credit, interest rate, and inflation risks.

Monitor changes in interest rates, credit spreads, and economic indicators to modify bond allocations to maximize portfolio returns.

3. Mutual funds:

Mutual funds are investment vehicles that combine money from several individuals to invest in a diverse portfolio of stocks, bonds, and other securities. Mutual funds are managed by professional fund managers who make investment choices on behalf of their clients. Individual investors like mutual funds for their diversity, expert management, and simplicity.

Considerations:

Choose mutual funds depending on your investment goals, asset class, investing style, and expense ratio.

When selecting mutual funds for your portfolio, consider fund performance, management tenure, turnover rate, and risk-adjusted returns.

Diversify among mutual fund categories and investing strategies to get broad market exposure while reducing single-fund risk.

4. Exchange-traded funds (ETFs):

Exchange-traded funds (ETFs) are similar to mutual funds but trade on stock exchanges alongside individual equities. ETFs monitor indexes, sectors, commodities, or other asset classes and attempt to mimic their performance. ETFs, unlike conventional mutual funds, provide diversity, flexibility, and low fees, making them attractive investment vehicles for both regular and institutional investors.

Considerations:

Choose ETFs according to asset class, investment purpose, underlying index, and fee ratio.

Assess liquidity, trading volume, bid-ask spread, and tracking errors while trading ETFs on stock exchanges.

Diversify between ETFs and asset classes to get broad market exposure while reducing single-ETF risk.

5. Real estate investment trusts (REITs):

Real estate investment trusts (REITs) are corporations that own, manage, or finance income-producing real estate holdings. REITs provide exposure to the real estate market without the requirement to own actual assets. Investors benefit from REITs via rental revenue, capital appreciation, and dividend payouts. The many forms of REITs offered to investors include publicly listed REITs, private REITs, and mortgage REITs.

Considerations:

Compare REITs based on property type, geographical location, occupancy rates, rental revenue, and dividend yield.

When deciding on REITs for your portfolio, consider their fundamentals, property portfolios, leverage ratios, and managerial skills.

Diversify among REIT sectors, such as residential, commercial, industrial, and healthcare, to mitigate risk and capitalize on opportunities in the real estate market.

6. Alternative investments:

Alternative investments include a diverse group of non-conventional assets and investing techniques that differ from typical equities, bonds, and cash. Alternative investments provide diversity, have a low correlation with conventional asset classes, and have the potential to provide good risk-adjusted returns. Investors might examine alternative investments such as hedge funds, private equity, venture capital, commodities, and cryptocurrency.

Considerations:

Consider alternative investments depending on investment strategy, risk-return profile, liquidity, and regulatory requirements.

Before investing in alternative investment funds, consider the fund managers' track record, investment skills, and fee structure.

Diversify your portfolio by allocating a part of it to alternative assets, which may minimize volatility and perhaps increase total returns.

Conclusion:

Choosing proper investment vehicles and alternatives is critical for developing a diverse investment portfolio that is consistent with your financial objectives, risk tolerance, and investing strategy. When putting up your portfolio, take into account the features, dangers, and prospective returns of various investment possibilities. Diversify among asset classes, sectors, and investment techniques to disperse risk and capitalize on opportunities across the financial landscape. Monitor your portfolio regularly and make changes as appropriate to ensure that it is well-diversified and in line with your investing goals and risk tolerance. With careful preparation and intelligent investment vehicle selection, you may create a robust investment portfolio that can help you achieve long-term financial success.

Chapter 9: Retirement Planning.

Retirement planning is an important part of financial management that needs thoughtful study and smart decision-making. In this chapter, we will look at the significance of defining retirement goals and how to create clear and attainable goals for your retirement years.

9.1 Set Retirement Goals

Retirement objectives form the core of your retirement planning strategy. They give guidance, incentives, and a framework for making sound financial and lifestyle choices in retirement. Setting retirement goals includes examining your present financial circumstances, visualizing your ideal retirement lifestyle, and developing realistic goals for achieving your retirement desires. Here are some important factors to consider when creating retirement goals:

Understanding your current financial situation:

Before creating retirement objectives, it's critical to assess your existing financial situation. Examine your income, spending, assets, debts, savings, and investments to determine where you stand financially. Examine your retirement assets, such as 401(k), IRAs, pensions, and Social Security payments, to establish your retirement preparedness and predict income streams in retirement. Consider your age, job position, health, and family circumstances while evaluating your financial condition.

Imagine Your Retirement Lifestyle:

Take time to consider your desired retirement lifestyle and what it implies. Consider your interests, hobbies, passions, and retirement goals. Consider where you want to live, how you want to spend your time, and what hobbies you want to pursue after retirement. Consider your retirement objectives in terms of travel, leisure, volunteering, family time, and personal satisfaction. Painting a realistic picture of your retirement goals may help you better connect your financial objectives with your desired lifestyle.

Determine your retirement age:

Determine the age at which you want to retire and move from full-time employment to retirement. When deciding on your retirement age, take into account your work path, health, longevity, and financial preparation. Determine if you want to retire early, at the standard retirement age, or continue to work part-time after retirement. Your retirement age will affect your retirement savings objectives, income requirements, and investment strategy.

Estimating retirement expenses:

Estimate your retirement expenditures and determine how much money you will need to cover your living expenses in retirement. Consider the costs of housing, healthcare, utilities, transportation, food, insurance, taxes, and discretionary expenditures. To ensure that your retirement income is enough to sustain your chosen level of life over time, consider inflation and anticipated healthcare expenditures. Use retirement calculators, and budgeting tools, or talk with a financial counselor to correctly estimate your retirement needs.

Establishing Financial Goals:

Set precise retirement financial objectives based on your lifestyle, age, and expected costs. Determine how much you need to save for retirement, how to divide your retirement savings across different investment vehicles, and how to earn retirement income from a variety of sources. Set quantifiable goals for your retirement savings, investment returns, and retirement income so that you can monitor your progress and adjust your approach as needed. Consider using milestones, checkpoints, or deadlines to hold yourself responsible and motivated to reach your retirement objectives.

Accounting for risks and contingencies:

Prepare for possible risks and contingencies that might affect your retirement goals, including market volatility, unanticipated spending, health difficulties, longevity risk, and inflation. Build flexibility into your retirement plan to help you adjust to changing circumstances and overcome unexpected problems. Consider obtaining insurance, setting up emergency reserves, or diversifying your assets to defend against unexpected catastrophes and preserve financial stability in retirement.

Review and revise your goals:

Regularly assess and adjust your retirement objectives to account for changes in your living circumstances, financial condition, and retirement prospects. Update your objectives as you approach retirement, go through important life events, or review your priorities and values. Maintain flexibility and open-mindedness throughout your retirement planning process, and be prepared to change your objectives and tactics as required to remain on track to achieve your retirement goals.

Setting clear, practical, and attainable retirement objectives allows you to map out your retirement planning path and take proactive measures toward a safe and satisfying retirement future. To ensure a smooth transition into retirement, invest time and effort in identifying your retirement objectives, seeking advice from financial specialists or retirement planners, and remaining dedicated to them. With careful preparation and intelligent goal-setting, you may enjoy the retirement lifestyle you've always desired while living your senior years with confidence and peace of mind.

9.2 Retirement Account Options (401k, IRA, etc.)

Setting objectives is just one aspect of retirement planning; you must also carefully analyze the many retirement account alternatives accessible to you. These accounts are used to save and invest money expressly for retirement, and they provide tax breaks as well as the possibility for future gain. In this part, we will look at the most popular retirement account choices, such as 401(k)s, IRAs, and other alternatives, and analyze their features, advantages, and concerns.

401(k) Plans:

A 401(k) plan is an employer-sponsored retirement savings account that enables workers to put a percentage of their pre-tax salary into a tax-deferred investment account. Traditional 401(k) contributions are made using pre-tax cash, which reduces your taxable income in the year of the contribution. Contributions grow tax-deferred until they are withdrawn in retirement and taxed as regular income. Many workplaces provide matching payments, which may considerably increase your retirement savings.

Features and benefits:

Tax-deferred growth: Contributions and investment profits accumulate tax-free until withdrawal.

Employer matching: Some businesses provide matching contributions, which essentially double your retirement savings.

Contribution restrictions: The IRS establishes yearly contribution limits that might vary according to age and income level.

Investment alternatives: Most 401(k) plans include a variety of investment options, including mutual funds, index funds, and target-date funds.

Portability: If you move employment, you may transfer your 401(k) money to an IRA or another employer's retirement plan.

Considerations:

Vesting schedule: Employer contributions may be subject to a vesting schedule, which means you may not completely own them until you have worked for the firm for a certain number of years.

Early withdrawal penalties: Withdrawing from a 401(k) before age 59½ may result in a 10% penalty, in addition to income taxes.

RMDs: Starting at age 72 (or 70 ½ if attained before January 1, 2020), you must begin drawing RMDs from your regular 401(k), subject to income tax.

Individual Retirement Accounts (IRAs)

An individual retirement account (IRA) is a tax-advantaged retirement savings account that anybody may create and contribute to, regardless of their job. There are two kinds of IRAs: regular and Roth.

Traditional IRA:

Contributions to a conventional IRA may be tax deductible, depending on your salary and if you are covered by a workplace retirement plan.

Investment profits are tax-deferred until withdrawn.

Retirement withdrawals are subject to normal income taxation.

RMDs start at age 72 (or 70 ½ if you turned 70 ½ before January 1, 2020).

Roth IRAs:

Contributions to a Roth IRA are paid after taxes, so they are not deductible.

Investment profits grow tax-free, and eligible withdrawals from retirement are tax-free.

There are income restrictions for contributing to a Roth IRA, but contributions may be made at any age as long as you make money.

There are no required minimum distributions (RMDs) during the account owner's lifetime.

Other retirement account options:

In addition to 401(k) plans and IRAs, some people have access to alternative retirement account choices, such as:

- Simplified Employee Pension (SEP) IRAs

Savings Incentive Match Plan for Employees (SIMPLE) IRAs.

Solo 401(k) programs for the self-employed

Health Savings Accounts (HSAs) and a qualifying high-deductible health plan (HDHP)

These accounts have distinct features, contribution limitations, and eligibility restrictions, so it's critical to understand the details of each choice and how they fit into your overall retirement planning approach.

Conclusion:

Choosing the appropriate retirement account(s) is an important step in your retirement planning process. When choosing retirement plans that meet your financial objectives and preferences, take into consideration employer offers, tax consequences, investment possibilities, contribution restrictions, and withdrawal requirements. Maximize your retirement account contributions to take advantage of tax breaks and long-term growth opportunities. Consult with a financial adviser or tax specialist to assess your possibilities and create a retirement savings plan that is suited to your specific requirements and circumstances. With careful planning and disciplined saving and investing, you may create a strong retirement portfolio that will give you financial stability and peace of mind in your senior years.

9.3 Strategy for Retirement Savings

Retirement planning requires smart savings and investments to achieve a happy and secure retirement lifestyle. In this part, we will look at numerous retirement savings techniques that may help you establish a large nest egg and meet your retirement objectives.

1. Start early and save consistently.

One of the most effective retirement savings strategies is to start early and save regularly. The force of compounding allows your savings to expand over time, so the sooner you start saving, the longer your money has to grow. Make retirement savings a top priority by setting up automatic payments to accounts like 401(k), IRAs, and other retirement savings vehicles. Consistently contribute a proportion of your monthly salary, even if it is little, and gradually raise your payments as your income and financial position allow.

2. Take advantage of employer matching contributions:

If your workplace provides a retirement savings plan, such as a 401(k), make full use of any matching contributions available. Employer matching contributions are effectively free money that may greatly increase your retirement savings. Contribute a sufficient amount to your employer-sponsored retirement plan to maximize the employer's matching contributions. Consider it part of your pay package, and take advantage of it to boost your retirement savings.

3. Maximize your contributions to tax-advantaged retirement accounts:

Maximize contributions to tax-advantaged retirement accounts, such as 401(k), IRAs, or Roth IRAs, to benefit from the tax breaks and potential for long-term development. Contribute the maximum permissible amount to your retirement accounts each year, taking into consideration the IRS' contribution restrictions. Traditional retirement funds allow for tax-deferred growth, allowing your contributions to grow tax-free until withdrawn, whereas Roth accounts allow for tax-free withdrawals in retirement, giving you more tax-planning freedom.

4. Use Catch-Up Contributions:

If you're 50 or older, take advantage of the IRS's catch-up contributions to increase your retirement savings. Catch-up contributions enable older people to make extra payments to their retirement accounts beyond the standard contribution restrictions. For example, in 2021, those over the age of 50 may make catch-up contributions of up to $6,500 to their 401(k) plans and $1,000 to their IRAs, in addition to the usual contribution limitations.

5. Diversify your investments:

Diversify your retirement assets among asset types, such as equities, bonds, and cash equivalents, to reduce risk and increase rewards. When deciding on investments for your retirement accounts, keep your risk tolerance, investing goals, and time horizon in mind. Choose an asset mix that is consistent with your financial objectives and offers a balance of growth potential and downside protection. Regularly examine and rebalance your investment portfolio to ensure diversity, and modify your asset mix as required to reflect changing market circumstances.

6. Delay retirement and continue working:

Consider postponing retirement and working beyond the usual retirement age to increase your retirement funds and Social Security benefits. Working longer helps you save more money, postpone withdrawals from your retirement accounts, and perhaps improve your Social Security payments by postponing claims until later in life. Furthermore, being active and involved in the workplace may provide cerebral stimulation, social connection, and a sense of purpose after retirement.

7. Downsize and simplify your lifestyle:

Downsizing and simplifying your lifestyle is another retirement savings method that may help you save more money by lowering your costs. Evaluate your existing spending patterns to find areas where you might save money or remove unneeded purchases. Consider downsizing your house, selling unnecessary stuff, or lowering discretionary spending on non-essential purchases. Living below your means and adopting a modest lifestyle may help you raise your savings rate and expedite your path to retirement.

8. Prepare for Healthcare Costs and Long-Term Care:

When budgeting for retirement, remember to include healthcare and long-term care expenditures. Healthcare bills may be a big expense in retirement, particularly as you get older and need more medical care. Consider obtaining long-term care insurance to protect yourself against the high expenses of long-term care services like nursing home care or home healthcare. Budget for healthcare expenses in your retirement plan, and look into Medicare supplementary insurance options to fill coverage gaps that Medicare does not provide.

Conclusion:

Implementing successful retirement savings techniques is critical for accumulating a sizable nest egg and attaining financial independence in retirement. To maximize your retirement savings, start saving early, invest regularly, and take advantage of tax-advantaged retirement accounts and employer-matching contributions. Diversify your assets, postpone retirement if feasible, and simplify your lifestyle to save costs and boost savings. Plan for healthcare and long-term care expenditures to ensure you're ready for any unforeseen medical demands in retirement. By using these techniques and being disciplined in your savings and investing strategy, you may create a strong retirement portfolio that will give you financial stability and peace of mind in your golden years.

Chapter 10: Real Estate Investment

10.1 Real Estate Investment Basics

Real estate investing is a popular wealth-building strategy that provides several prospects for income generation, equity growth, and portfolio diversification. In this part, we'll go over the fundamentals of real estate investing, such as distinct investment techniques, important considerations, and possible rewards and hazards.

Understanding Real Estate Investments:

Real estate investment is the acquisition, ownership, management, rental, or sale of real estate to create income or capital appreciation. Real estate assets include a diverse variety of properties, such as residential residences, commercial structures, industrial facilities, retail spaces, multifamily apartments, and unoccupied land. Investors may choose from a variety of real estate investing techniques, each of which provides distinct possibilities and possible profits.

Key Factors for Real Estate Investing:

Before getting into real estate investing, it's important to grasp the fundamental aspects and elements that might influence your investment decisions:

1. Market Analysis: Conduct extensive market research and analysis to uncover potential investment opportunities, as well as evaluate market trends, supply and demand dynamics, property valuations, rental rates, and economic indicators. When examining market circumstances, consider geography, demography, employment growth, infrastructural development, and the regulatory environment.

2. Financial study: Conduct a thorough financial study of possible real estate investments to determine their revenue potential, costs, cash flow estimates, financing choices, and return on investment (ROI). Calculate important financial parameters such as net operating income (NOI), cap rate, cash-on-cash return, internal rate of return (IRR), and return on investment (ROI) to determine the investment's profitability and viability.

3. Risk Management: Determine and reduce the risks involved with real estate investment, such as market risk, property risk, financing risk, liquidity risk, interest rate

risk, tenant risk, and regulatory risk. Diversification, due diligence, insurance coverage, contingency planning, and legal compliance are all risk management measures that may help preserve your investment money and reduce possible losses.

4. Investment plan: Determine your investment plan and goals, such as generating rental income, capital appreciation, fixing and flipping properties, developing new construction projects, or investing in real estate crowdfunding, or REITs. Customize your investing plan to reflect your financial objectives, risk tolerance, investment horizon, and real estate market knowledge.

5. Financing possibilities: Learn about various financing possibilities for real estate ventures, such as traditional mortgages, government-insured loans, private financing, hard money loans, seller financing, and innovative financing arrangements. Consider the cost of borrowing, loan terms, interest rates, down payment requirements, and loan-to-value (LTV) ratios to find the best financing choice for your investment goals and financial position.

Benefits of Real Estate Investment:

Real estate investment has a variety of potential benefits for investors, including:

1. Revenue Generation: Rental properties may provide a consistent stream of rental revenue, which can be used to supplement passive income and cover property bills, mortgage payments, and operational costs.

2. Appreciation Potential: Real estate holdings have the potential to increase in value over time, enabling investors to accumulate equity and generate capital gains when selling at a higher price than the original purchase price.

3. Portfolio Diversification: Real estate investments provide diversification advantages by exposing investors to a distinct asset class that has a low connection with conventional equities and bonds, therefore spreading risk and lowering portfolio volatility.

4. Tax Advantages: Real estate investors can benefit from a variety of tax breaks, such as depreciation deductions, mortgage interest deductions, property tax deductions, capital gains tax deferrals, and tax-deferred exchanges, which can boost after-tax returns and overall investment performance.

5. Inflation Hedge: Real estate investments may act as a hedge against inflation by providing a physical asset that increases in value over time, retaining buying power, and functioning as a dependable store of value in inflationary circumstances.

Risks of Real Estate Investing:

While real estate investment has high potential rewards, it also carries several risks and problems, including:

1. Market Risk: Real estate values are influenced by market swings, economic cycles, interest rate changes, and geographical variables, which may all have an impact on property prices, rental demand, and investment returns.

2. Property Risk: Real estate properties may suffer maintenance expenditures, repair charges, vacancy losses, tenant turnover, property damage, and unanticipated liabilities, all of which may affect cash flow and profitability.

3. Financing Risk: Leveraged real estate investments include borrowing money to fund property acquisitions, which exposes investors to financing risk, default risk, foreclosure risk, and interest rate risk, especially during economic downturns or increasing interest rates.

4. Operational Risk: Effectively managing rental properties involves time, effort, experience, and resources for tenant interactions, property upkeep, lease agreements, legal compliance, and property management obligations.

5. Liquidity Risk: Real estate investments are generally illiquid when compared to other asset classes, making it difficult to sell properties quickly or access investment cash in times of financial need, necessitating cautious preparation and exit plans.

Conclusion:

Real estate investment provides several chances and possible rewards for individuals looking to accumulate wealth, produce income, and attain financial independence. Understanding the fundamentals of real estate investing, conducting extensive research and analysis, and implementing sound investment strategies and risk management techniques allow investors to capitalize on the lucrative opportunities presented by the real estate market while minimizing potential risks and maximizing investment returns. Whether you're a first-time investor or a seasoned real estate expert, real estate investment can be a satisfying and successful endeavor when done with research, dedication, and strategic thinking.

10.2 Rental Properties vs. Real Estate Investment Trusts (REITs)

Real estate investment provides investors with a variety of opportunities to gain exposure to the real estate industry while also generating income or capital gains. Real Estate Investment Trusts (REITs) and rental properties are two popular investment possibilities. In this part, we will compare and contrast rental properties and REITs, focusing on their characteristics, advantages, risks, and investment implications.

Rental properties:

Rental properties are residential or commercial properties that are purchased to rent out to tenants to produce rental income and perhaps gain wealth over time. Here are some significant characteristics and concerns for rental properties:

Ownership and Control:

Rental property investors own and control the properties they acquire, enabling them to make choices about property management, tenant selection, rent pricing, and property upkeep.

Investors may manage their rental properties themselves or employ property managers to handle day-to-day operations and tenant interactions.

Income Potential:

Rental properties can provide consistent rental revenue, which may serve as a dependable source of passive income and cover property expenditures, mortgage payments, and operational costs.

Rental income may offer cash flow stability and long-term wealth building, particularly if the properties are in high-demand rental areas with high rental demand and rental appreciation potential.

Appreciation and Equity Buildup:

Rental properties have the potential to increase in value over time, enabling investors to accumulate equity and generate capital gains when they sell for a greater price than the purchase price.

Mortgage amortization allows investors to gradually create equity in their rental properties by paying down the mortgage principal, increasing their ownership share.

Tax benefits:

Rental property owners may benefit from a variety of tax breaks, such as depreciation deductions, mortgage interest deductions, property tax deductions, and capital gains tax deferral, which may lower taxable income and increase total investment returns.

Tax breaks may boost after-tax cash flow and increase the tax efficiency of rental property investments, offering extra incentives to real estate investors.

Liquidity and management effort:

Rental properties are extremely illiquid assets in comparison to other asset types, necessitating time, effort, and resources to efficiently acquire, sell, and manage them.

Managing rental properties entails continuing obligations like property upkeep, tenant management, lease agreements, rent collection, and legal compliance, all of which may take time and either hands-on engagement or the use of property management services.

Real Estate Investment Trusts (REITs):

REITs are publicly listed businesses that own, operate, or finance income-producing real estate assets, enabling investors to acquire exposure to the real estate market via shares of REIT stocks. Here are some significant characteristics and concerns for REITs:

Diversity and accessibility:

REITs provide investors with an easy and accessible alternative to investing in real estate without physically owning physical properties, while also providing diversification advantages by investing in a portfolio of assets across multiple industries, geographies, and property types.

REIT shares may be purchased and sold on stock exchanges like individual stocks, giving investors the liquidity and flexibility they need to join or leave real estate investments quickly.

Income Distribution:

REITs are obliged by law to deliver a considerable amount of their taxable profits to shareholders in the form of dividends, providing investors with a consistent stream of dividend income that may exceed that of other dividend-paying equities or bonds.

REIT dividends are normally paid quarterly and may offer investors both passive income and long-term capital appreciation.

Professional Management:

REITs are professionally managed by qualified real estate professionals who handle property acquisition, management, leasing, financing, and asset sales on behalf of their investors.

Investors benefit from professional managerial skills, industry knowledge, and economies of scale, which may improve operational efficiency and investment returns.

Liquidity and transparency:

REIT shares are highly liquid assets that may be purchased and sold on stock exchanges at market prices, giving investors the freedom and flexibility to alter their real estate holdings as required.

REITs are subject to regulatory scrutiny and reporting requirements, ensuring the openness and disclosure of financial information, operational performance, and investing activities for investors.

Tax considerations:

REIT dividends may be taxed differently from conventional stock dividends, with some being categorized as ordinary income, qualified dividends, or returns of capital, depending on the REIT's revenue sources and distribution strategy.

REIT investors may benefit from tax-efficient arrangements and preferential tax treatment over direct real estate ownership, including possible tax deferral and tax-advantaged retirement funds.

Conclusion:

Both rental properties and REITs are attractive choices for investors looking for real estate exposure as well as potential income or capital gain. Each investment option has unique characteristics, advantages, dangers, and concerns, and the decision between rental properties and REITs is based on personal preferences, investment goals, risk tolerance, and financial circumstances. Before making an investment choice, investors should carefully weigh the benefits and drawbacks of rental properties and REITs, undertake extensive due diligence, and examine their investment objectives and preferences. Diversifying their real estate assets and mixing rental properties with REIT investments allows investors to create a well-balanced real estate portfolio that matches their long-term investment goals and improves overall investment performance.

10.3 Maximizing Returns on Real Estate

Real estate investment has the potential to generate significant profits via rental revenue, property appreciation, and a variety of value-added initiatives. In this part, we will look at tactics for optimizing profits on real estate investments, such as property selection, financing choices, rental management, value-added enhancements, and exit plans.

1. Property selection:

Selecting the correct property is critical for optimizing profits from real estate investments. When looking at investment homes, consider the following factors:

Location: Look for homes in favorable areas with high rental demand, easy access to amenities, excellent schools, low crime rates, and the opportunity for long-term growth.

Property Type: Consider various property kinds, such as single-family houses, multifamily apartments, commercial buildings, or mixed-use complexes, and choose assets that match your investment objectives and risk tolerance level.

Condition: Determine the property's condition and estimate repair expenditures, remodeling charges, and upkeep needs to maintain its viability as an investment.

Market Trends: Look at local market trends, supply and demand dynamics, rental rates, vacancy rates, and property prices to find investment possibilities and hazards.

2. Financing Options:

Choosing the correct financing solution will help you maximize your investment returns and leverage your resources efficiently. Consider these funding alternatives for real estate investments:

Conventional Mortgages: Use typical mortgage loans from banks or lenders to finance property acquisitions, leveraging your capital with borrowed cash and spreading the expense over time.

Government-Insured Loans: Look into government-backed lending programs like FHA, VA, and USDA loans, which provide advantageous terms, low down payment requirements, and competitive interest rates to qualified applicants.

Private Financing: Seek private financing from individuals, private lenders, or hard money lenders to finance real estate purchases, which offers more flexibility, speed, and less severe qualifying requirements than regular lenders.

Seller Financing: Negotiate seller financing agreements in which the seller serves as the lender and funds a part of the property's purchase price, enabling you to buy properties with little upfront cash and advantageous conditions.

3. Rental management:

Efficient rental management is critical for increasing rental revenue, reducing vacancies, and preserving property values. For good rental management, use the following tactics:

Tenant Screening: Thoroughly screen potential renters to ensure that they are dependable, responsible, and financially secure enough to pay rent on time and properly maintain the property.

Lease Agreements: Use thorough lease agreements that clearly describe tenant duties, rent payment terms, lease length, maintenance requirements, and occupancy regulations to protect your rights and enforce lease conditions.

Rent collection: Implement effective rent collection systems, such as online payment platforms, automated withdrawals, or electronic transfers, to reduce late payments and delinquencies.

Property Maintenance: To attract and keep renters, and maintain properties regularly by conducting routine inspections, responding quickly to maintenance concerns, completing repairs and improvements as required, and ensuring premises are clean, safe, and well-maintained.

4. Value-Added Improvements:

Implementing value-added upgrades may boost property value, attract high-quality tenants, and increase rental revenue. Consider the following value-added real estate investing strategies:

Cosmetic Upgrades: To modernize houses and increase marketability, make cosmetic changes such as painting, flooring replacement, kitchen renovations, bathroom updates, and curb appeal enhancements.

Energy-Efficient Renovations: Invest in energy-efficient renovations such as insulation, HVAC systems, windows, lights, and appliances to save money on utilities, attract environmentally aware renters, and boost property value.

Amenities and Facilities: To distinguish homes and charge higher rentals, provide desired amenities and facilities such as laundry rooms, fitness centers, swimming pools, outdoor areas, parking, and security features.

Value-added chances: identify chances to increase rental revenue and property value by converting underused space, increasing rental units, subdividing properties, or repositioning assets.

5. Exit Strategy:

A clear exit strategy is critical for maximizing earnings and returns on real estate investments. When making real estate investments, consider the following exit strategies:

Long-Term Hold: Keep properties for a long time to benefit from rental income, property appreciation, mortgage payoffs, and tax breaks, enabling investments to compound and expand over time.

Fix and Flip: Buy distressed properties, remodel them to raise their value, and sell them for a profit quickly, taking advantage of market inefficiencies and value creation possibilities.

1031 Exchange: A 1031 exchange allows you to delay capital gains taxes by reinvesting revenues from property sales into like-kind replacement properties, preserving equity, and continuing to develop wealth via real estate investments.

Portfolio Diversification: To maximize returns and successfully manage risk, diversify your real estate portfolio by selling failing properties, reallocating money to higher-performing assets or alternative property types, and rebalancing your investment portfolio.

Conclusion:

Real estate investment returns must be maximized through thorough planning, smart decision-making, and rigorous implementation of investment strategies. Investors can maximize the potential of their real estate investments and achieve their financial objectives by selecting the right properties, effectively leveraging financing options, implementing efficient rental management practices, making value-added improvements, and executing well-defined exit strategies. Whether you're a first-time investor or a seasoned real estate expert, taking a proactive and methodical approach to real estate investment may help you optimize profits, manage risks, and develop long-term wealth through property ownership.

Crossing The Gap

Chapter 11: Entrepreneurship and Passive Income

11.1 Starting and Scaling Your Business

Entrepreneurship allows you to create passive income streams and achieve financial independence by establishing scalable enterprises that produce money without needing active participation. In this part, we will look at the process of beginning and expanding a firm, including conception, validation, execution, and expansion plans.

1. Ideation and conceptualization:

The process of launching a company starts with ideation and conceptualization, in which entrepreneurs discover market issues, requirements, or opportunities and create novel solutions or business concepts to meet them. Consider the following phases for idea generation and concept development:

Determine Market Gaps: Conduct market research and analysis to uncover unmet requirements, pain areas, or neglected market segments that provide the potential for company innovation and disruption.

Generate Ideas: Come up with company ideas, product concepts, or service offers that address recognized issues, meet market needs, or capitalize on new trends, technology, or consumer behavior.

Validate Concepts: Before investing in company development, do market research, customer input, and a feasibility study to analyze demand, viability, scalability, and revenue potential.

2. Business Plan and Execution:

Once a solid company concept has been found and verified, entrepreneurs must create a detailed business plan and implement successful methods to make their vision a reality. Consider the stages below for business strategy and execution:

Describe the Value Proposition: Clearly describe the unique value proposition, target market, customer segmentation, competitive advantages, and differentiation tactics that will position the company for success and market acceptability.

Create a scalable company model that includes revenue streams, cost structures, pricing strategies, distribution networks, customer acquisition approaches, and growth predictions to ensure long-term income and profitability.

Create an actionable execution plan that includes precise targets, milestones, timetables, and resource allocation techniques for successfully guiding company launch, operations, marketing, sales, and growth efforts.

Create a Minimum Viable Product (MVP) or prototype to test and verify business ideas, get customer input, iterate on product features, and fine-tune business processes before expanding operations.

3. Growth Strategy and Scaling:

To achieve long-term development and profitability, a corporation must scale its operations, extend its market reach, and increase its income sources. Consider the following growth and scaling tactics:

Customer Acquisition: Use digital marketing, content marketing, social media advertising, search engine optimization (SEO), email marketing, influencer alliances, and referral programs to acquire, engage, and retain consumers.

Product Innovation: To remain competitive, relevant, and unique in the marketplace, continuously reinvent goods, services, or solutions in response to market feedback, technological breakthroughs, industry trends, and changing consumer demands.

Strategic Partnerships: Create strategic alliances, collaborations, or partnerships with similar firms, industry leaders, distributors, suppliers, or influencers to utilize resources, broaden market reach, and accelerate development via synergistic interactions.

Scalable Operations: Streamline company operations, automate repetitive processes, improve workflows, and use technology, tools, or software solutions to boost productivity, save costs, and grow operations without losing quality or customer experience.

Funding and Investment: Look into funding possibilities such as bootstrapping, angel investors, venture capital, crowdfunding, or small company loans to generate funds for business growth, product development, marketing activities, or infrastructure improvements to support scaling operations.

4. Observation and adaptation:

Entrepreneurs must monitor key performance indicators (KPIs), track metrics, and modify plans in response to market dynamics, consumer feedback, competitive pressures, and internal performance indicators as their businesses expand and develop. Consider the following strategies for monitoring and adaptation:

Performance Measurement: Develop key performance indicators (KPIs), metrics, and benchmarks to monitor company performance, measure progress toward objectives, and assess the success of growth plans, marketing campaigns, and operational activities

Data Analytics: Use data analytics, business intelligence tools, and analytics platforms to collect insights, evaluate trends, detect patterns, and make data-driven choices that improve company operations, enhance customer experiences, and drive revenue development.

Continuous Improvement: Create an organizational culture of continuous improvement, experimentation, and learning, fostering innovation, creativity, and flexibility to remain ahead of the curve, capitalize on opportunities, and reduce risks in a quickly changing business environment.

Conclusion:

Starting and growing a company is a difficult but rewarding process that involves vision, dedication, endurance, and strategic preparation. Entrepreneurs can build successful businesses that generate passive income, add value, and achieve long-term financial success by taking a systematic approach to entrepreneurship, identifying viable business opportunities, developing innovative solutions, effectively executing strategies, and adapting to market dynamics. Whether you're a seasoned entrepreneur or an aspiring startup founder, entrepreneurship provides endless opportunities to generate passive income, pursue your passion, and make a great impact on the world via company innovation and entrepreneurship.

11.2 Generate Passive Income Streams

Passive income streams are sources of income that take little work to sustain and produce ongoing money over time. In this section, we will examine a variety of techniques and methods for producing passive income through business, investments, and other income-creating activities.

1. Real estate investments:

Rental properties, real estate crowdfunding, REITs, and other investment vehicles all provide prospects for passive income generation. Consider the following passive income options for real estate:

Rental Properties: Invest in residential or commercial rental properties and receive rental income from tenants, which can help you create equity, produce cash flow, and accumulate wealth over time.

Real Estate Crowdfunding: Join real estate crowdfunding platforms that pool investor money to finance real estate projects, generating passive income via rental revenue, loan repayments, or property appreciation.

Real Estate Investment Trusts (REITs): Invest in publicly listed REITs that own, operate, or finance income-producing real estate assets, receiving dividends on rental income and capital growth while avoiding direct property ownership or management duties.

2. Dividend investing:

Dividend investing is the act of buying dividend-paying stocks, mutual funds, or exchange-traded funds (ETFs) and collecting passive income via monthly dividend payments from the company's revenues. Consider the following dividend investment strategies:

Dividend Stocks: To optimize passive income, invest in established firms with a track record of steady profitability, robust cash flows, and reliable dividend payments. Focus on dividend-growth stocks or high-yield dividend stocks.

Dividend Funds: Invest in dividend-focused mutual funds or exchange-traded funds (ETFs) that hold diverse portfolios of dividend-paying companies from various sectors, geographies, and market capitalizations, offering exposure to both dividend income and capital appreciation.

3. Online Businesses and Digital Assets:

Online enterprises and digital assets provide prospects for passive revenue generation via e-commerce, affiliate marketing, digital goods, and content development. Consider the following methods for generating passive income online:

E-commerce sites: Set up and create e-commerce sites that sell physical, digital, or drop shipping items, using platforms like Shopify, Amazon FBA, or Etsy to automate order fulfillment, payment processing, and customer care.

Affiliate Marketing: Promote affiliate goods or services using websites, blogs, social media, or email marketing to make passive income via affiliate commissions on sales or leads created by referral links.

Digital Products: Create and sell e-books, online courses, software apps, templates, or digital downloads on platforms such as Udemy, Teachable, Gum Road, or Click Bank to make passive income from product sales and recurring subscriptions.

Content Monetization: Use platforms like YouTube, Twitch, Patreon, or Sub stack to monetize content production efforts via advertising revenue, sponsorships, memberships, or donations, generating passive money from ad impressions, sponsorships, or viewer contributions.

4. Peer-to-peer lending and crowdfunding:

Peer-to-peer lending and crowdfunding platforms allow people to lend money to borrowers or invest in projects while generating passive income via interest payments or investment returns. Consider these passive revenue methods for peer-to-peer lending and crowdfunding:

Peer-to-Peer Lending: Join peer-to-peer lending platforms that link borrowers and investors and receive passive income from interest payments on personal loans, business loans, or real estate loans financed via the platform.

Crowdfunding Investments: Invest in crowdfunding campaigns or projects on platforms like Kickstarter, Indiegogo, or Seed Invest to help entrepreneurs, artistic initiatives, or real estate developments while generating passive income via investment returns, royalties, or revenue-sharing agreements.

5. Royalties and licensing:

Individuals may generate passive income by licensing their intellectual property, creative works, or proprietary assets to other parties in return for royalties or licensing fees. For royalties and licensing, consider these passive revenue methods:

Intellectual Property: License patents, trademarks, copyrights, or trade secrets to firms, manufacturers, or publishers to generate passive revenue via royalty or licensing fees depending on product sales, use, or distribution.

Creative Works: License music, artwork, photography, writing, or video material to media businesses, publishers, or streaming platforms to generate passive revenue via royalties from sales, downloads, or use rights.

6. Automated Systems and Technology

Individuals may produce passive income via internet enterprises, digital goods, or affiliate marketing by using automated methods and technological solutions such as artificial intelligence and software platforms. Consider the following passive income techniques that use automated processes and technology:

Automated Online Companies: Create and develop online companies on autopilot by using automated systems, processes, and workflows to produce passive income from sales, subscriptions, and advertising revenue.

Software as a Service (SaaS): Create and sell software products, mobile applications, or digital tools as subscription-based services to generate passive revenue via periodic subscription fees, use charges, or license agreements.

Affiliate Marketing Platforms: Build affiliate marketing platforms, comparison websites, or referral networks to automate affiliate marketing campaigns, monitoring, and commissions, enabling users to make passive income via affiliate referrals and commissions.

Conclusion:

Creating passive income streams via business, investments, and other income-generating activities provides prospects for financial independence, asset building, and lifestyle flexibility. Individuals may generate several streams of passive income by diversifying their income sources, using passive income tactics, and establishing scalable enterprises or investment portfolios. Whether you're a new entrepreneur, an experienced investor, or an aspiring digital nomad, passive income may help you achieve your financial objectives, pursue your hobbies, and live life on your terms.

11.3 Managing Risks and Rewards in Entrepreneurship

Entrepreneurship is a journey full of possibilities, difficulties, risks, and rewards. Balancing risks and benefits are critical for entrepreneurs to make educated choices, handle uncertainty, and succeed in their business ventures. In this part, we will look at the risk-reward dynamics in entrepreneurship as well as ways for efficiently managing and limiting risks while maximizing possible gains.

Understanding Risk in Entrepreneurship:

Entrepreneurship entails a variety of hazards, including financial, commercial, operational, and regulatory risks, among others. Understanding and detecting risks is critical for entrepreneurs as they analyze possible threats, foresee problems, and devise risk mitigation techniques. Here are some typical hazards in entrepreneurship:

Financial Risks: Financial risks include the possibility of capital loss, cash flow issues, debt buildup, bankruptcy as a result of insufficient financing, bad financial management, or unanticipated costs.

Market risks are caused by changes in market circumstances, consumer preferences, competitive dynamics, or industry trends that influence product demand, pricing strategies, sales predictions, and revenue forecasts.

Operational risks are caused by internal causes such as operational inefficiencies, supply chain interruptions, manufacturing delays, quality control concerns, or workforce shortages, all of which have an impact on corporate operations and performance.

Legal and regulatory risks arise from noncompliance with laws, rules, or industry standards, exposing organizations to legal penalties, fines, litigation, or reputational harm.

Evaluating Potential Reward:

While entrepreneurship entails dangers, it also provides chances for financial gain, personal satisfaction, and professional development. Assessing prospective rewards enables entrepreneurs to discover the incentives, motives, and goals that drive their entrepreneurial activities. Here are some possible incentives for entrepreneurs:

Financial Rewards: Profits, revenues, dividends, or capital gains from successful company operations, investments, or entrepreneurial initiatives may be used to build wealth and achieve financial freedom.

Independence and Autonomy: Entrepreneurship provides entrepreneurs with freedom, autonomy, and control over company choices, strategies, and operations, enabling them to follow their vision, passion, and innovative ideas without limitations.

Personal satisfaction: Entrepreneurship offers chances for personal satisfaction, self-expression, and aspirational fulfillment, allowing entrepreneurs to follow their passions, interests, and values via purpose-driven initiatives.

influence and legacy: By establishing enterprises, products, or programs that enhance lives, empower communities, or drive social change, entrepreneurs may have a positive influence, address societal issues, and leave a long-lasting legacy.

Strategies to Balance Risks and Rewards:

Balancing risks and benefits in entrepreneurship require proactive risk management, strategic planning, and flexible decision-making. Implementing risk mitigation measures allows entrepreneurs to reduce exposure to possible dangers while increasing prospects for rewards. Here are several approaches to balancing risks and benefits in entrepreneurship:

Conduct risk assessments: identify, evaluate, and prioritize possible risks linked with business endeavors, investments, or entrepreneurial activities, taking into account their probability, effect, and mitigating variables.

Diversify Income Sources: Spread the risk by diversifying income streams, revenue sources, or company lines, reducing reliance on a single source of income or market segment, and improving resistance to economic downturns or industry upheavals.

Develop Resilience: Create financial reserves, emergency funds, or contingency plans to withstand unforeseen occurrences, economic downturns, or company losses, creating a buffer against financial hardship and maintaining corporate continuity.

Implement Lean Practices: Lean methods, agile frameworks, or iterative approaches to company development may help entrepreneurs test ideas, verify concepts, and iterate on plans rapidly and affordably.

Stay Informed and Adaptive: Stay current on market trends, industry developments, technical improvements, and regulatory changes, and adjust tactics and business models appropriately to maximize opportunities and manage risks.

Seek mentorship and direction: Seek mentorship, counsel, or direction from experienced entrepreneurs, industry experts, or business consultants who can provide insights, perspectives, and knowledge to help you manage problems, make educated choices, and succeed.

Conclusion:

Balancing risks and benefits are an essential component of entrepreneurship, requiring careful thinking, strategic planning, and disciplined execution. Entrepreneurs may succeed in their business ventures by assessing possible risks, estimating potential benefits, and successfully executing risk management measures. While entrepreneurship entails risks and obstacles, it also provides opportunities for financial gain, personal satisfaction, and professional development. Entrepreneurs may traverse the changing terrain of entrepreneurship, follow their ideas, and generate long-term influence and value in the world by adopting an entrepreneurial attitude, developing resilience, and using resources and support networks.

Crossing The Gap

Chapter 12: Tax Planning and Optimization.

12.1: Understanding tax laws and regulations

Tax planning and optimization are critical components of financial management because they help people and corporations reduce tax bills, enhance tax efficiency, and improve their overall financial situation. In this section, we will examine the foundations of tax laws and regulations, preparing readers to navigate the complex terrain of taxes successfully.

1. The Importance of Tax Knowledge:

Understanding tax laws and regulations is crucial for people and organizations seeking to comply with legal obligations, reduce tax loads, and improve financial results. Taxation affects many elements of personal and corporate finances, such as income, investments, assets, deductions, credits, and estate planning. Taxpayers who understand tax rules may make better judgments, take advantage of tax breaks, and improve their financial situation.

2. Components of Tax Systems:

Tax systems vary per jurisdiction, including various kinds of taxes, laws, rates, and administrative processes. Tax systems typically involve the following components:

Income taxes are levied on people, businesses, or other organizations based on their income, profits, or earnings from a variety of sources, including wages, salaries, investments, and business operations.

Capital Gains Taxes: Taxes charged on the sale or disposal of capital assets such as stocks, bonds, real estate, or company assets based on the asset's acquisition price less its selling price.

Property taxes are assessments of the value of real property, personal property, or assets held by people, companies, or other entities and are often collected by local governments to pay for public services and infrastructure.

Sales taxes: taxes imposed on the sale of products or services, collected by merchants or service providers and paid to government agencies, which vary by jurisdiction and are applied at the point of sale.

Excise Taxes: Taxes charged on certain commodities, services, or activities, such as alcohol, tobacco, fuel, or luxury items, are often applied at the manufacturer, importer, or consumer levels.

Estate and Inheritance Taxes: Taxes levied on the transfer of wealth, assets, or property from one person to another by death or inheritance, subject to specific exemptions, thresholds, and rates.

3. Tax planning strategies:

Tax planning includes making strategic decisions and taking proactive steps to reduce tax bills, improve financial results, and achieve particular tax-related goals. Effective tax preparation tactics include the following:

Income Deferral: Deferring income to future years or spreading it out over many years using retirement savings, deferred compensation programs, or installment sales to decrease current tax bills and benefit from lower future tax rates.

Deduction Maximization: Making the most of permissible deductions, credits, exemptions, and tax benefits by meticulous planning, documentation, and adherence to tax regulations, such as deductions for mortgage interest, charitable donations, education, medical, and business costs.

Retirement Savings: Use retirement savings vehicles like 401(k) plans, Individual Retirement Accounts (IRAs), Roth IRAs, or SEP-IRAs to postpone taxes on contributions, grow assets tax-deferred, and possibly get tax-free payments in retirement.

Tax-efficient Investment Strategies: Using tax-loss harvesting, asset location, portfolio rebalancing, and long-term investment holdings to reduce capital gains taxes, increase after-tax returns, and optimize investment outcomes.

Entity Structuring: Choosing the right business form, such as sole proprietorships, partnerships, corporations, or limited liability companies (LLCs), to reduce taxes, safeguard assets, and improve company operations based on criteria including liability, taxation, ownership, and management.

Estate Planning: Using measures such as gifting, trusts, life insurance, or charity planning to reduce estate taxes, protect wealth, and make it easier to transfer assets to heirs or beneficiaries in an efficient and tax-effective manner.

4. Compliance and reporting requirements:

Taxpayers are obligated to follow tax rules and regulations, keep correct records, and report to government authorities. Common compliance and reporting obligations include the following:

Filing Tax Returns: Individuals, corporations, and other organizations must submit tax returns every year, disclosing income, deductions, credits, and other pertinent information to appropriately determine tax obligations.

Taxpayers must pay taxes owing to government authorities by the due dates indicated in tax legislation, including anticipated tax payments, withholding taxes, or payroll taxes, to avoid fines, interest, or enforcement proceedings.

Recordkeeping: Taxpayers must retain organized and accurate records of financial transactions, receipts, invoices, statements, and other paperwork supporting income, spending, deductions, credits, and tax positions for auditing and compliance with tax regulations.

Reporting Requirements: To prevent tax evasion, money laundering, or fraud, taxpayers may be required to report specific transactions, investments, or activities to government authorities, such as foreign bank accounts, cryptocurrency transactions, offshore assets, or large financial transactions.

Conclusion:

Understanding tax rules and regulations is critical for people and organizations to properly manage tax complexities, reduce tax bills, and improve financial results. By learning about tax systems, applying strategic tax planning techniques, and adhering to legal requirements, taxpayers may improve their financial well-being, protect their wealth, and accomplish their long-term financial objectives. Whether you are an individual taxpayer, a small company owner, or a corporate executive, proactive tax planning and compliance are critical components of healthy financial management and asset preservation in today's dynamic and ever-changing tax landscape.

12.2 Tax-Efficient Investing Strategy

Tax-efficient investing is an important part of financial planning because it allows individuals to maximize after-tax returns, reduce tax obligations, and optimize their investment portfolios. In this section, we will look at numerous tax-efficient investment techniques that individuals and organizations can use to improve their financial performance while reducing the burden of taxes.

1. Asset location:

Asset location is the strategic placement of assets in various kinds of investment accounts to reduce taxes and increase after-tax earnings. By taking into account the tax treatment of different investment vehicles and asset types, investors may optimize their portfolio structure for tax efficiency. Key factors for asset location include the following:

Tax-Advantaged Accounts: Contribute as much as possible to tax-advantaged retirement accounts such as 401(k) plans, Individual Retirement Accounts (IRAs), Roth IRAs, or Health Savings Accounts (HSAs) to take advantage of tax-deferred growth, tax deductions (for traditional accounts), or tax-free withdrawals (for Roth accounts).

Taxable Brokerage Accounts: Place tax-efficient investments such as index funds, exchange-traded funds (ETFs), or tax-managed mutual funds in taxable brokerage accounts to reduce taxable distributions, capital gains, or dividend income, as these investments typically have lower turnover and generate fewer taxable events.

Tax-Exempt Accounts: To produce tax-free interest income, consider investing in tax-exempt municipal bonds or municipal bond funds inside taxable accounts, particularly for investors in higher tax brackets or those looking to diversify fixed-income holdings while reducing tax obligations.

2. Tax Loss Harvesting:

Tax-loss harvesting is the sale of stocks at a loss to offset capital gains and decrease taxable income, resulting in lower total tax obligations. This technique enables investors to capitalize on investment losses while preserving portfolio diversity and market exposure. Key factors for tax-loss harvesting are:

Capital Gains and Losses: Identify assets with unrealized losses and sell them to realize capital losses, which may then be used to offset capital gains achieved elsewhere in the portfolio, lowering net capital gains liable to tax.

Wash Sale Rules: Follow wash sale rules, which restrict repurchasing the same or nearly similar securities within 30 days before or after the sale date, to maintain tax conformity and avoid capital loss disallowance.

Strategic Planning: Use tax-loss harvesting strategically throughout the year to maximize tax advantages, adjust portfolio allocations, and effectively manage tax obligations, taking into account market circumstances, investment goals, and individual tax situations.

3. Dividend reinvestment plans (DRIPs):
Dividend reinvestment plans (DRIPs) enable investors to automatically reinvest dividends into new shares of the same investment, allowing for compound growth and deferring taxes on reinvested profits until they are sold. DRIPs provide tax-efficient compounding advantages and are particularly beneficial for long-term investors looking to reinvest earnings without immediate tax repercussions.

4. Tax-advantaged investments:
Invest in tax-advantaged or tax-exempt assets that provide preferential tax treatment, tax deferral, or tax-free income, lowering tax obligations while increasing after-tax profits. Examples of tax-advantaged investments are:
Municipal Bonds: Invest in municipal bonds issued by state or local governments, which provide tax-exempt interest income at the federal and, in certain cases, state levels, offering a source of tax-free income for high-income investors.
Qualified Opportunity Zones: Consider investing in Qualified Opportunity Zones (QOZs) through Qualified Opportunity Funds (QOFs) to take advantage of tax deferral, reduction, or elimination of capital gains taxes on investments in designated economically distressed areas, subject to specific requirements and timelines outlined in tax regulations.
Real Estate: Use tax-advantaged real estate investment structures like Real Estate Investment Trusts (REITs), 1031 exchanges, or Opportunity Zone real estate investments to produce tax-advantaged income, deductions, or deferrals from real estate ownership or investment.

5. Tax-efficient Withdrawal Strategies:
To reduce taxes and maximize income distributions at retirement or other stages of life, carefully plan withdrawal methods. Consider these tax-efficient withdrawal strategies:
Tax-Bracket Management: Manage withdrawals from retirement funds to remain in lower tax brackets and avoid being taxed at higher rates, using progressive tax brackets and optimizing withdrawal timing and sequencing depending on individual tax circumstances.
Roth Conversion Strategies: Consider converting traditional retirement account assets to Roth accounts using Roth conversions, which allow investors to pay taxes on

converted amounts at current tax rates and potentially receive tax-free withdrawals in retirement, thereby reducing tax liabilities and increasing tax flexibility.

Required Minimum Distributions (RMDs): Plan RMDs from retirement funds strategically to comply with IRS laws while reducing taxes, taking into consideration age, life expectancy, account balances, and distribution alternatives to maximize retirement income and tax results.

Conclusion:
Tax-efficient investing techniques are critical for maximizing after-tax returns, reducing tax obligations, and improving long-term investment results. Investors can improve their financial well-being, preserve wealth, and achieve their investment goals by implementing asset location strategies, tax-loss harvesting, dividend reinvestment plans, tax-advantaged investments, and tax-efficient withdrawal strategies, all while successfully navigating the complexities of taxation. Whether you're an individual investor, a retirement saver, or a wealth manager, tax-efficient investing is a critical component of sound financial planning and asset management. It allows individuals to develop and protect wealth while following their financial goals and ambitions.

12.3: Reducing Tax Liabilities for Long-Term Wealth

Minimizing tax payments is critical for people and organizations seeking long-term prosperity and financial stability. Taxpayers may save more money for future generations by using smart tax planning methods and maximizing tax-efficient structures. In this section, we'll look at a variety of ways and strategies for reducing tax payments to encourage long-term wealth growth and financial success.

1. Comprehensive tax planning:
Comprehensive tax planning involves assessing all aspects of an individual's or business's financial situation to identify tax optimization opportunities and reduce tax obligations in areas such as income, investments, assets, and estate planning. Key components of comprehensive tax planning are:

Income Tax Strategies: Use retirement contributions, health savings accounts (HSAs), flexible spending accounts (FSAs), and other tax-favored accounts and perks to reduce taxable income, maximize deductions and credits, and optimize tax rates.

Investment Tax Methods: Use tax-efficient investment vehicles, asset allocation methods, and tax-loss harvesting procedures to reduce capital gains, dividend income, and tax drag in investment portfolios while increasing after-tax returns and compounding growth.

Asset Protection Strategies: Place assets and investments in tax-efficient corporations, trusts, or vehicles to protect them from excessive taxes, creditor claims, or unfavorable legal proceedings, protecting wealth and providing financial stability for future generations.

Estate Tax Strategies: Strategically manage estate transfers, gifts, and bequests to reduce estate taxes, generation-skipping taxes, or inheritance taxes using trusts, lifetime gifts, charity contributions, and other estate planning approaches to ensure efficient asset transfer and preservation.

2. Tax-efficient Investments:

Invest in tax-efficient assets, funds, or methods that provide advantageous tax treatment, deferral, or exemption, enabling investors to reduce tax payments while increasing after-tax gains in the long run. Examples of tax-efficient investments are:

Tax-Advantaged Retirement Accounts: Contribute as much as possible to tax-deferred retirement accounts such as 401(k) plans, IRAs, Roth IRAs, or SEP-IRAs to defer taxes on contributions, grow investments tax-free, and potentially access tax-free distributions in retirement, maximizing retirement savings and tax deferral benefits.

Municipal Bonds: Invest in tax-exempt municipal bonds issued by state or local governments, which provide tax-free interest income at the federal and, in certain cases, state levels. This is a source of tax-free income for investors looking to reduce tax obligations on fixed-income assets.

Tax-Managed Funds: Consider investing in tax-managed mutual funds or exchange-traded funds (ETFs) that use tax-efficient strategies like low turnover, selective trading, and capital gains deferral to reduce taxable distributions and capital gains, resulting in higher after-tax returns for investors.

Qualified Opportunity Zones (QOZs): Consider investing in Qualified Opportunity Zones (QOZs) through Qualified Opportunity Funds (QOFs) to take advantage of tax deferral, reduction, or elimination of capital gains taxes on investments in designated economically distressed areas, allowing for tax-efficient growth and investment diversification.

3. Tax-Advantaged Structures:

Tax-advantaged structures, companies, or vehicles can help increase tax efficiency, lower tax loads, and protect wealth for long-term development and financial stability. Examples of tax-advantaged structures are:

Limited Liability Companies (LLCs): Form an LLC for business operations, real estate investments, or asset holding to take advantage of pass-through taxation, limited liability protection, and tax treatment flexibility, which optimizes tax efficiency and asset protection for entrepreneurs and investors.

Trusts: Establish trusts such as revocable living trusts, irrevocable trusts, charitable trusts, or dynasty trusts to manage assets, reduce estate taxes, avoid probate, and facilitate wealth transfer and preservation across generations, resulting in efficient estate planning and asset protection for families and beneficiaries.

Family Limited Partnerships (FLPs): Create FLPs for estate planning, wealth transfer, or asset protection to consolidate assets, centralize management, and take advantage of valuation discounts for gifting and transfer tax purposes. This allows for tax-efficient wealth preservation and succession planning for family businesses and estates.

4. Tax-Friendly Strategies:

Use tax-advantaged tactics and approaches to maximize tax breaks, deductions, and incentives while lowering tax obligations and compliance risks. Examples of tax-favored schemes are:

Charitable Giving: Donate to qualifying charitable organizations, donor-advised funds, or charitable trusts to earn tax breaks on charitable donations, decrease taxable income, and promote philanthropic causes while accomplishing tax-efficient wealth management and social impact goals.

Health Savings Accounts (HSAs): Contribute to an HSA to earn tax deductions for qualifying medical expenditures, grow investments tax-free, and withdraw cash tax-free for eligible medical expenses, allowing individuals and families to save money while still receiving healthcare coverage.

Education Savings Plans: Invest in 529 plans, Coverdell Education Savings Accounts (ESAs), or prepaid tuition plans to benefit from tax-deferred growth, tax-free withdrawals for qualified education expenses, and state tax breaks for college savings. This ensures that children and beneficiaries receive tax-efficient education funding and tuition planning.

Conclusion:

Tax liability minimization is critical for people and organizations looking to develop long-term wealth, maintain financial stability, and fulfill their financial objectives and dreams. Taxpayers may optimize their tax situations, decrease tax loads, and maximize after-tax profits over time by executing comprehensive tax planning methods, investing in tax-efficient assets and structures, and taking advantage of tax-favored procedures and incentives. Whether you're an individual investor, business owner, or wealth manager, tax optimization is an important part of prudent financial management and wealth preservation. It allows taxpayers to create and preserve wealth while pursuing long-term financial goals and legacies.

: **Crossing The Gap**

Chapter 13: Overcoming Financial Setbacks

13.1 Strategies for Recovering from Financial Hardships

Financial setbacks are unavoidable in life, but they do not have to shape our financial destiny. Whether it's a job loss, unforeseen medical bills, or a market slump, managing financial difficulties needs fortitude, ingenuity, and smart thinking. In this part, we will look at successful ways of dealing with financial setbacks and restoring financial stability.

1. Assess the situation:

The first step in overcoming financial losses is to analyze the situation accurately. Take stock of your financial situation, including income, spending, debts, assets, and emergency funds. Understand the underlying reasons for the setback and find places where you can make quick improvements to improve your finances.

2. Create a budget:

Create a realistic budget using your existing income and expenses. Prioritize basic costs like housing, utilities, food, and transportation while cutting down on non-essential spending. Look for ways to cut prices, negotiate bills, or discover alternate methods to stretch your budget further.

3. Create an emergency fund:

An emergency fund is one of the finest ways to protect yourself against financial misfortunes. Begin establishing or refilling your emergency fund as soon as possible, even if it means beginning little. Aim to save three to six months' worth of living costs to protect against unforeseen catastrophes and offer a financial safety net.

4. Generate Additional Income:

Look for ways to augment your current income. Consider freelancing, part-time employment, the gig economy, or selling stuff you no longer need. Every additional dollar you make might help you meet costs, pay off debt, or save more quickly.

5. Prioritize debt repayment:

If you have debt, prioritize repayment to lower interest rates and improve your financial situation. Concentrate on high-interest debts first, such as credit card debt, and then investigate consolidation or refinancing alternatives to reduce interest rates. Pay your debts on time, and avoid taking on extra debt where possible.

6. Negotiate with the creditors:

If you are having difficulty meeting your financial responsibilities, do not hesitate to contact creditors and lenders to explore hardship solutions. Many creditors may work with you to adjust payment arrangements, cut interest rates, or even halt payments during tough circumstances. Be proactive in explaining your predicament and researching viable solutions.

7. Seek financial assistance:

Investigate government aid programs, community resources, and philanthropic groups that may provide financial help or relief to those in need. Look for organizations that provide aid with housing, utilities, healthcare, food, and other necessities to help bridge the gap during difficult times.

8. Focus on Financial Education

Invest in financial education to boost your financial knowledge and decision-making abilities. Take advantage of the free resources, seminars, courses, and counseling services provided by nonprofit organizations, community centers, and banks. Learn about budgeting, saving, investing, debt management, and other financial subjects to help you make more educated choices.

9. Stay positive and persistent:

Overcoming financial difficulties needs a good attitude, tenacity, and persistence. Maintain focus on your objectives, be adaptive to changing circumstances, and appreciate minor triumphs along the way. Remember that setbacks are just temporary obstacles, and with commitment and work, you can overcome them and emerge stronger than before.

10. Review and Adjust Regularly:

To stay on track for recovery, regularly examine your financial situation and change your methods as needed. Monitor your progress, keep track of your costs, and evaluate your objectives regularly to ensure you're making real progress toward financial security. To successfully overcome obstacles, be willing to make changes, seek help, and learn from your experiences.

Conclusion:

Financial setbacks are a normal part of life, but they do not have to ruin your financial future. You may overcome financial challenges and recover control of your finances by applying proactive methods, controlling spending, conserving money, and getting help when necessary. Remember that resilience, resourcefulness, and drive are essential for overcoming obstacles and attaining long-term financial success. With patience, dedication, and the appropriate techniques, you can overcome any challenge and create a better financial future for yourself and your loved ones.

13.2 Strengthening Resilience in the Face of Adversity

Financial setbacks may be intimidating and difficult, but growing resilience is essential for coming back stronger and more resilient than before. In this part, we will look at ways to develop resilience in the face of financial difficulty, allowing you to handle setbacks with bravery, resolve, and perseverance.

1. Cultivate a growth mindset.

Adopting a growth mindset is critical for developing resilience and conquering financial challenges. Accept setbacks as chances for development and learning, rather than as insurmountable hurdles. Believe in your capacity to adapt, learn, and endure in the face of adversity, knowing that setbacks are just temporary roadblocks on the way to achievement.

2. Practice self-compassion.

Practicing self-compassion and kindness toward oneself is critical during times of financial distress. Be patient and sympathetic with yourself, realizing the tension and emotions that may accompany financial failures. Treat yourself with the same care and compassion that you would show a friend experiencing comparable difficulties, and remember that setbacks do not determine your value or identity.

3. Develop social support networks:

During challenging times, rely on your support networks, which include family, friends, mentors, and community resources, to provide emotional and practical aid. Share your stories, seek advice, and accept assistance when provided, knowing that you are not alone in enduring financial difficulties. Surround yourself with good influencers who will inspire and support you on your path to resilience.

4. Develop coping strategies:

Identify appropriate coping techniques for dealing with stress, worry, and uncertainty caused by financial losses. Stay grounded and focused during difficult moments by practicing mindfulness, meditation, deep breathing exercises, or other relaxation methods. Engage in activities that provide you with pleasure, contentment, and a sense of purpose to improve your health and resilience.

5. Set realistic goals.

Set realistic and attainable objectives that are consistent with your beliefs, priorities, and resources, taking into account the existing conditions and limits. Break down huge ambitions into smaller, more doable stages, and celebrate your accomplishments along the way. Setting realistic objectives and milestones helps you retain a sense of direction, purpose, and drive in the face of failures and hurdles.

6. Increase Financial Literacy:

Invest in your financial literacy and knowledge to give yourself the ability to make educated choices and handle financial issues successfully. Learn about budgeting, saving, investing, debt management, and financial planning tools to boost your financial resilience and confidence. Seek out credible sources of information, attend workshops or seminars, and speak with financial specialists when required to improve your financial knowledge and abilities.

7. Embrace adaptability and flexibility.

Be versatile and flexible in your approach to addressing financial setbacks, acknowledging that circumstances may change and new possibilities may appear unexpectedly. To overcome problems and grab new possibilities for development and resilience, be willing to consider other ideas, adapt your plans, and pivot as needed.

8. Concentrate on What You Can Control:

Concentrate your efforts on parts of your financial condition over which you have control, such as your spending habits, saving practices, and investment selections. Take proactive actions to control spending, save for emergencies, and make smart financial choices that are consistent with your long-term objectives and beliefs. By concentrating on what you can manage, you may reclaim your feeling of power and agency over your financial destiny.

9. Practice gratitude and optimism.

Cultivate a grateful and optimistic attitude by concentrating on the good parts of your life, especially when faced with hardship. Express thanks for the benefits, opportunities, and support networks in your life, and foster optimism by picturing a greater future. By cultivating appreciation and optimism, you can build resilience and manage financial losses with hope.

10. Seek professional help:

Don't be afraid to seek professional help from financial advisers, counselors, or therapists, who may provide advice, knowledge, and support customized to your specific needs and situations. A financial expert can assist you in creating a specific

strategy for overcoming financial setbacks, managing stress, and reaching long-term financial objectives with confidence and resilience.
Conclusion:

Developing resilience in the face of financial losses needs bravery, commitment, and self-compassion. By establishing a growth mindset, building social support networks, creating coping methods, setting realistic objectives, and accepting adaptation, you may handle financial adversities with resilience and emerge stronger and more resilient than ever before. Remember that setbacks are just temporary roadblocks on the route to development and success, and with tenacity, persistence, and the correct techniques, you can overcome any barrier and create a better financial future for yourself and your loved ones.

13.3 Seeking Professional Help as Needed

Financial setbacks may be intimidating, and dealing with them alone may not always be the best option. Seeking professional assistance, when necessary, may provide vital support, direction, and knowledge in helping you overcome obstacles and recover financial security. In this part, we will look at why it is important to seek professional help amid financial difficulties, as well as the sorts of specialists that may provide essential assistance.

1. Financial advisers:

Financial advisers are specialists who may provide individualized advice and experience to help you negotiate financial issues, create objectives, and build strategies for financial success. A financial adviser may give impartial counsel and suggestions targeted at your specific financial position and objectives, whether you're struggling with debt, budgeting, investing, or retirement planning.

2. Credit counselors:

If you're dealing with debt or credit, credit counselors can help you create a strategy to manage your debt, improve your credit score, and attain financial stability. Credit counseling firms provide counseling sessions, debt management programs, and financial education materials to help people overcome debt and restore control of their money.

3. Bankruptcy attorneys:

In times of extreme financial trouble, bankruptcy lawyers may provide legal advice and representation to those contemplating bankruptcy as a debt relief option.

Bankruptcy lawyers may examine your financial status, explain your bankruptcy rights and alternatives, and walk you through the bankruptcy process, allowing you to make educated decisions about your financial future.

4. Tax Pros:

Tax specialists, such as certified public accountants (CPAs) or enrolled agents (EAs), may provide useful advice on tax planning, preparation, and settlement. Whether you're dealing with tax debt, IRS audits, or complicated tax issues, tax specialists can give expert advice, negotiate with tax authorities on your behalf, and help you manage tax laws and regulations successfully.

5. Legal advisors:

In cases involving legal disputes, contracts, or financial agreements, legal advisers may provide legal advice and representation to preserve your rights and interests. Legal advisers may give legal advice, evaluate papers, and represent you in discussions or legal actions, including landlord-tenant difficulties, foreclosure proceedings, or contractual disputes.

6. Mental health professionals:

Financial setbacks may hurt your mental health and well-being, causing stress, worry, and sadness. Therapists and counselors may provide emotional support, coping skills, and treatments to help you manage stress, process emotions, and develop resilience during challenging situations.

7. Community resources:

In addition to professional services, there are community resources and organizations that may help those who are struggling financially. Nonprofit groups, community centers, and government agencies may provide financial assistance, food, housing support, or job opportunities to assist people in overcoming immediate obstacles and gaining access to important services.

8. Support groups:

Joining support groups or peer-led networks may also provide essential assistance and encouragement amid financial difficulties. Support groups, whether online or in person, provide a secure environment for people to share their experiences, seek advice, and be encouraged by others who have encountered similar issues. Connecting with individuals who understand your circumstances may give you a feeling of community and solidarity as you fight to overcome financial obstacles.

Conclusion:

Seeking professional assistance when you are experiencing financial difficulties is not a sign of weakness but rather a proactive step toward regaining control of your money and reaching financial stability. Whether you need financial guidance, debt counseling, legal representation, or emotional support, there are people and services available to help you overcome financial obstacles. Remember that you do not have to face financial difficulties alone, and obtaining professional assistance may give you the knowledge, skills, and support you need to overcome obstacles and establish a stronger financial future.

Crossing The Gap

Chapter 14: Economic Change and Market Volatility

14.1 Adapting to Economic Changes

Change is unavoidable in today's dynamic global economy. Economic upheavals and market volatility may have serious consequences for people, companies, and the economy as a whole. Adapting to these changes needs tenacity, vision, and strategic preparation. In this part, we will look at the necessity of responding to economic fluctuations and how to efficiently navigate market turbulence.

Understanding Economic Shifts

Economic shifts are changes in economic circumstances, such as swings in GDP growth, inflation, interest rates, employment, and consumer spending. These changes may be impacted by a variety of variables, including geopolitical events, technical breakthroughs, monetary policies, and global market patterns.

Factors causing economic shifts:

1. Geopolitical Events: Political instability, trade disputes, and geopolitical conflicts may all affect economic circumstances by influencing investor confidence, trading connections, and market dynamics.

2. Technological Innovations: Advances in technology, automation, and digitalization have the potential to disrupt sectors, offer new possibilities, and transform economic landscapes.

3. Monetary Policies: Central bank policies, such as interest rate changes and quantitative easing, have the potential to impact borrowing costs, investment choices, and total economic activity.

4. Demographic Changes: Population growth, aging demographics, and migration patterns may all influence labor markets, consumer behavior, and long-term economic trends.

Strategies for Adjusting to Economic Changes:

1. Diversification entails diversifying your income streams, assets, and company operations to limit exposure to certain economic risks while also capitalizing on varied possibilities.

2. Flexibility: Remain adaptable and nimble in reacting to changing economic situations, altering strategy, reallocating resources, and capitalizing on new possibilities.

3. Implement risk management methods, such as hedging, insurance, and contingency planning, to reduce the effect of economic uncertainty and market volatility.

4. Embrace innovation and adapt to technological changes to increase competitiveness, generate growth, and capitalize on new market trends.

5. Education and Skill Development: Invest in ongoing education, training, and skill development to remain relevant in changing sectors and increase employability in dynamic labor markets.

6. Long-Term Planning: Take a long-term approach to financial and company planning, emphasizing sustainable development, value creation, and resistance to economic cycles.

7. Networking and Collaboration: Establish strong networks, partnerships, and collaborations to capitalize on collective knowledge, resources, and skills while managing economic transitions and market issues.

8. Monitoring and Analysis: Stay up to date on economic data, market trends, and industry changes.

Navigating market volatility:

Market volatility is defined as swings in asset values, stock markets, and financial instruments caused by shifting investor moods, economic variables, and external events. While market volatility may cause uncertainty and concern, it also provides chances for profit, value investment, and long-term wealth building.

Strategies for Navigating Market Volatility:

1. Asset Allocation: Diversify your portfolio among asset types, such as equities, bonds, real estate, and commodities, to disperse risk and decrease market volatility.

2. Implement a dollar-cost averaging technique by investing regular sums of money at specified times, independent of market circumstances, to smooth out swings and eliminate timing risks.

3. Value investment: Prioritize basic research, intrinsic value, and long-term growth possibilities over short-term market swings or speculative fads in your value investment strategy.

4. Risk Tolerance Assessment: Determine your risk tolerance, investing objectives, and time horizon to ensure that your investment plan is in line with your financial goals and degree of comfort in dealing with market volatility.

5. Maintain an emergency fund with enough cash to meet living costs, unforeseen expenditures, and financial commitments amid market downturns or economic uncertainty.

6. Long-Term Focus: When investing, have a long-term perspective in mind, concentrating on quality firms, solid fundamentals, and sustainable growth prospects rather than short-term market swings or speculative transactions.

7. Opportunistic Investing: Use market downturns and volatility to buy undervalued assets, stocks, or real estate at a discount, taking advantage of brief market disruptions and mispricing.

8. Emotional Discipline: When managing assets during times of market volatility, use emotional discipline, patience, and resilience to prevent knee-jerk responses, panic selling, or illogical conduct motivated by fear or greed.

Conclusion:

Adapting to economic fluctuations and dealing with market volatility are critical abilities for people, firms, and investors seeking long-term financial success and stability. Understanding the sources of economic change, employing adaptive tactics, and taking a disciplined approach to investing can allow you to manage risks, capitalize on opportunities, and traverse complex economic landscapes with confidence and foresight. Remember that economic fluctuations and market volatility are unavoidable parts of the investing process, and with strategic preparation, adaptability, and resilience, you may succeed in dynamic and ever-changing markets.

14.2 Thriving Under Volatile Market Conditions

Market volatility is an unavoidable part of investment that is influenced by a variety of variables, ranging from economic data to geopolitical developments. While volatility may cause fear and uncertainty, it also provides an opportunity for savvy investors to succeed. In this part, we will look at tactics for not just surviving but prospering in unpredictable market situations.

Understanding market volatility:

Market volatility describes the frequency and amplitude of price movements in financial markets. Economic data releases, geopolitical concerns, company earnings reports, and market moods may all contribute to this phenomenon. Volatility is assessed by indices such as the VIX (Volatility Index), which may affect asset values in stocks, bonds, commodities, and currencies.

Strategies for Thriving in Volatile Markets:

1. Maintain a long-term view: In turbulent markets, it is critical to have a long-term view. Instead of responding quickly to short-term swings, focus on your financial goals and time horizon. Remember that volatility is frequently fleeting, and investing long-term may help you weather market ups and downs.

2. Divide Your Portfolio: Diversification is an essential approach for risk management in turbulent markets. Reduce concentration risk by diversifying your assets across asset classes, industries, and geographic locations. Diversification may help mitigate the effect of volatility on your portfolio and increase risk-adjusted returns over time.

3. Rebalance regularly: Market volatility might lead asset allocations to deviate from their intended weights. Rebalance your portfolio regularly to ensure it is in line with your strategic asset allocation goals. Selling overperforming assets and purchasing underperforming assets might help you maintain your desired risk profile while also capitalizing on market swings.

4. Focus on Quality Investments: In unpredictable markets, quality often shines. Concentrate on investing in high-quality firms with strong foundations, durable business strategies, and proven track records of success. Quality investments may be better suited to withstand market volatility and generate long-term rewards.

5. Stay Informed but Avoid Overreacting: Stay up-to-date on market movements, economic indicators, and geopolitical events, but don't overreact to breaking news or noise. Maintain a disciplined approach to investing based on research, analysis, and a thorough knowledge of your investment thesis.

6. Seek Out Opportunistic Buying Opportunities: Savvy investors may capitalize on volatile markets. Keep an eye out for market dips or corrections, since they may provide appealing entry chances for high-quality assets at lower costs. When values become enticing, prepare to invest funds opportunistically.

7. Embrace dollar-cost averaging: Dollar-cost averaging is a disciplined investment approach in which you invest a certain amount of money at regular intervals, regardless of market circumstances. This strategy may help mitigate the effect of market volatility by purchasing more shares when prices are low and fewer shares when prices are high, thereby decreasing the average cost per share over time.

8. Maintain Adequate Liquidity: In turbulent markets, liquidity is crucial. Ensure that you have enough cash reserves or liquid assets to cover your short-term financial demands, and take advantage of any investment opportunities that emerge. Having cash on hand may provide you with peace of mind and flexibility while managing market concerns.

9. Manage Your Emotions: Emotional control is essential in turbulent markets. Avoid making financial choices out of fear or greed, and instead, take a sensible and disciplined approach to investing. Focus on your long-term financial objectives and adhere to your investing strategy, regardless of short-term market swings.

10. Consider Alternative Assets: Diversify your portfolio by including alternative assets like real estate, commodities, private equity, or hedge funds. Alternative investments may have distinct risk-return profiles and a low correlation with standard asset classes, giving additional diversification advantages in turbulent market circumstances.

Conclusion:

While market volatility may be unnerving, it also creates possibilities for investors who are willing to negotiate uncertainty with fortitude and discipline. You may survive and prosper in tumultuous market circumstances by keeping a long-term view, diversifying your portfolio, concentrating on quality assets, and being disciplined in your approach. Remember that volatility is a normal aspect of investment, and by using the appropriate tactics and mentality, you may set yourself up for long-term financial success and resilience.

14.3 Investment Strategy for Uncertain Times

Investing in unpredictable times requires a deliberate strategy and a strategic attitude. Economic developments and market volatility may provide both problems and opportunities for investors, necessitating adaptive techniques to traverse choppy seas. In this part, we'll look at investing techniques designed to assist investors in making educated choices in the face of economic uncertainty and market volatility.

Assessing risk tolerance:

Before executing any investing plan, it is critical to determine your risk tolerance and investment goals. Consider your time horizon, financial objectives, liquidity requirements, and tolerance level for volatility. Understanding your risk tolerance can help you pick investing methods that are appropriate for your tastes and circumstances.

Diversification:

Diversification is a key component of wise investment, particularly during difficult times. Diversify your assets across asset classes, sectors, industries, and geographic locations to decrease concentration risk and the effect of volatility on your portfolio. In the long run, diversification may help smooth returns and enhance risk-adjusted performance.

Focus on quality:

In uncertain times, excellent assets often outperform. Invest in high-quality firms that have solid foundations, robust business strategies, and a track record of success. Look for firms with competitive advantages, long-term growth potential, and strong balance sheets that can withstand economic downturns and market volatility.

Long-term Perspective:

When investing during uncertain times, keep a long-term view in mind. Avoid responding rashly to short-term market volatility or trying to time the market. Instead, concentrate on your long-term financial goals and investing objectives, and stick to your investment strategy through market ups and downs. Remember, investing is a marathon, not a sprint, and patience is essential for success.

Opportunistic Purchases:

Market downturns and volatility may provide purchasing opportunities for astute investors. Keep an eye out for inexpensive assets or industries that may be momentarily out of favor but have promising long-term potential. Consider opportunistically allocating cash to purchase excellent assets at reduced rates, taking advantage of market disruptions and mispricing.

Income generation:

In uncertain times, income-generating assets may offer security and cash flow throughout market turbulence. Consider investing a part of your portfolio in income-producing assets like dividend-paying equities, bonds, real estate investment trusts (REITs), and high-quality fixed-income instruments. These investments may offer a consistent source of income while also reducing portfolio volatility during tumultuous market situations.

Active risk management:

Implement active risk management measures to safeguard your portfolio against negative outcomes and volatility. Use stop-loss orders, hedging measures, or options strategies to control risk and reduce possible losses during market downturns. Regularly examine and rebalance your portfolio to ensure that your planned asset allocation and risk exposure remain consistent with changing market circumstances.

Stay informed and adaptable:

Stay up-to-date on market changes, economic data, and geopolitical events that may impact investing markets. Keep up with shifting trends, rising dangers, and emerging possibilities, and be ready to adjust your investing plans accordingly. Maintain a fluid and adaptable attitude toward investing, altering your strategy when market circumstances change.

Get professional advice:

Consider getting professional counsel from financial planners, wealth managers, or investment specialists who may provide specialized guidance and expertise based on your specific requirements and circumstances. A trained adviser can assist you in navigating unpredictable times, building a well-diversified portfolio, and making educated investing choices that are consistent with your financial objectives and risk tolerance.

Conclusion:

Investing in unpredictable times requires a disciplined strategy, a strategic attitude, and an emphasis on long-term fundamentals. Diversifying your portfolio, concentrating on quality assets, keeping a long-term view, and employing active risk management measures can help you weather economic shifts and market turbulence with confidence and resilience. Remember to be educated, and adaptable, and seek expert assistance when necessary to make sound investing choices and accomplish your financial objectives in unpredictable times.

Crossing The Gap

Chapter 15: Lifestyle Design and Personal Fulfillment.

15.1: Define Your Ideal Lifestyle

In today's fast-paced world, finding personal satisfaction and creating a lifestyle that reflects your beliefs, ambitions, and goals is more vital than ever. In this chapter, we will look at how to define your ideal lifestyle, what is most important to you, and how you might live a life filled with pleasure, satisfaction, and purpose.

Understanding lifestyle design:

Lifestyle design is the deliberate process of shaping your life to match your beliefs, priorities, and personal preferences. It entails determining what is genuinely important to you, articulating your objectives and desires, and making deliberate decisions to create a life that is consistent with your vision of pleasure and satisfaction.

Reflection on Your Values:

The first step in designing your ideal lifestyle is to consider your fundamental values and beliefs. What ideals drive your choices and actions? What's most important to you in life? Take some time to reflect and determine the values that are most important to you, whether they be family, health, profession, relationships, personal development, or community participation.

Clarifying your priorities:

After you've defined your values, choose your priorities and objectives for each aspect of your life. What are your main priorities in terms of work, relationships, health, money, and personal growth? Rank them in order of priority and evaluate how you may devote your time, energy, and resources to achieving these objectives.

Visualizing your ideal life:

Visualization is a great technique for achieving your dream lifestyle. Spend some time visualizing your perfect life in great detail. Imagine yourself enjoying your ideal life, filled with love, contentment, and plenty in all aspects. Using your imagination, build a clear and appealing image of the life you wish to lead.

Identifying Key Element:

Next, define the fundamental characteristics that make up your ideal lifestyle. This might include things like your ideal living situation, work or business goals, relationships, hobbies and interests, health and wellness routines, and personal development opportunities. Consider which hobbies, events, and settings provide you with the greatest pleasure and satisfaction.

Setting SMART Goals:

Once you've determined your ideal lifestyle, develop SMART objectives to make it a reality. Specific, measurable, achievable, relevant, and time-bound are the characteristics of SMART goals. Break down your big vision into smaller, more manageable actions, and create milestones to measure your progress toward your ideal lifestyle.

Make conscious choices:

Designing your perfect lifestyle requires deliberate decisions that are consistent with your vision and aspirations. Evaluate your present habits, routines, and commitments to see whether they support or impede your intended lifestyle. Be ready to let go of anything that no longer serves you to create new chances and experiences that correspond with your goals.

Developing a Plan of Action:

Once you've determined your ideal lifestyle and objectives, devise a strategy to make your vision a reality. Determine the particular processes, resources, and support systems required to accomplish your objectives, and create a timeframe for execution. As you embark on your lifestyle design journey, be adaptable and open to changes.

Embracing growth and adaptation:

Lifestyle design is a continuous process of development, adaptation, and self-discovery. Be open to new experiences, possibilities, and problems that may occur along the journey. Accept change as a normal aspect of life, seeing it as a chance for growth, learning, and personal development.

Cultivating gratitude and mindfulness:

Finally, develop appreciation and awareness as you plan your ideal lifestyle. Take time to appreciate the joys, opportunities, and experiences that improve your life daily. Mindfulness may help you be present in the moment and enjoy the simple pleasures of daily life, regardless of the circumstances.

Conclusion:

Defining your ideal lifestyle is a very personal and inspiring process that starts with self-awareness, clarity, and purpose. By establishing your values, clarifying your priorities, picturing your ideal life, creating SMART objectives, and making mindful decisions, you can create a life that provides you with pleasure, satisfaction, and personal fulfillment. Remember that lifestyle design is a continuous process of development and adaptation, so be willing to embrace change and uncover new opportunities along the way. With dedication, bravery, and imagination, you can design a life that represents your inner nature and enables you to live genuinely and completely.

15.2 Balancing Financial Goals and Personal Values

Personal satisfaction entails more than simply financial achievement; it necessitates matching your financial objectives with your innermost beliefs and desires. In this chapter, we'll look at the necessity of balancing financial objectives with personal values, as well as how to combine the two to live a life of purpose, meaning, and satisfaction.

Understanding personal values:

Personal values are the concepts, beliefs, and ideals that influence your life choices, behaviors, and priorities. They reflect what is most important to you on a basic level and influence your attitudes, habits, and aspirations. Personal values include integrity, honesty, compassion, family, health, personal development, creativity, and community participation.

Identifying Financial Goals:

Financial goals are specific objectives regarding your financial well-being and security. They might include things like saving for retirement, buying a house, paying off debt, sponsoring your children's education, establishing a company, touring the globe, or reaching financial independence. Financial objectives give a road map for managing your money and living the lifestyle you want.

Aligning Financial Goals and Personal Values:

To live a life of personal satisfaction, you must link your financial objectives with your ideals. This includes ensuring that your financial choices and activities are in line with what is most important to you on a deeper level. For example, if family is your primary value, you may prioritize family activities over material things or pleasures.

Reflection on Core Values:
Take some time to think about your basic principles and how they connect to your financial objectives. Ask yourself questions like these:
Which values are most important to me?
How do my financial objectives align with my basic values?
Am I spending money in line with my values?
Do my financial choices contribute to my general well-being and fulfillment?
Prioritizing value-based spending:
Once you've determined your values and financial objectives, prioritize values-based spending that reflects what's most important to you. This means devoting your financial resources to activities, experiences, and purchases that improve your life and add to your sense of purpose and fulfillment. For example, you may decide to invest in experiences such as travel, education, or personal development that reflect your values of exploration, learning, and growth.
Setting Intentional Financial Goals:
When defining financial objectives, be sure they are consistent with your values and ambitions. Consider how each objective improves your total well-being and contentment, both in the short and long term. Set objectives that are consistent with your beliefs and represent what you want to accomplish in life, rather than pursuing external success indicators or cultural norms.
Making Conscious Financial Decisions:
Make conscious and purposeful financial decisions that reflect your beliefs and goals. Before making a purchase or financial commitment, consider if it is consistent with your underlying beliefs and adds to your overall feeling of contentment. By matching your purchasing patterns to your beliefs, you may build a more meaningful and happy relationship with money.

Looking for Financial Freedom and Flexibility:
Strive for financial independence and flexibility so that you can live according to your principles and pursue your hobbies and interests. Financial independence gives you the ability and resources to make decisions based on what is most important to you, rather than being influenced by financial limits or commitments. Create a financial foundation that supports your preferred lifestyle and allows you to live genuinely and completely.
Cultivating gratitude and contentment:
Finally, cultivate gratitude and satisfaction in your financial path, acknowledging the riches and benefits in your life, regardless of your financial situation. Practice thankfulness for the small pleasures, connections, and experiences that offer you joy

and contentment, and remember that genuine prosperity goes beyond material belongings and financial success.

Conclusion:

Balancing financial objectives with personal beliefs is critical to living a life of purpose, meaning, and contentment. You matching your financial choices with what is most important to you on a deeper level, you may have a more meaningful and rewarding relationship with money, resulting in more happiness and fulfillment in all aspects of your life. Remember that personal satisfaction comes from living by your beliefs, following your interests, and building a sense of purpose and meaning that goes beyond financial success.

15.3 Promoting Happiness and Well-Being Beyond Money

While financial security is essential for a comfortable existence, genuine contentment, and happiness go beyond material prosperity. In this part, we'll look at ways to nurture pleasure and well-being in areas other than money, giving your life meaning, purpose, and joy.

Understanding the nature of happiness:

Happiness is a broad notion that includes emotional well-being, life satisfaction, and a sense of purpose. It is impacted by a variety of elements other than monetary prosperity, including relationships, health, personal development, and a sense of purpose. Positive psychology research implies that internal elements, such as thinking, attitudes, and actions, are more important than external conditions in determining happiness.

Promoting Meaningful Relationships:

The quality of your connections is one of the most important factors in determining your happiness and well-being. Make significant ties with family, friends, and community members who encourage and inspire you. Invest time and work in cultivating these relationships, emphasizing deep, true connections above superficial exchanges. Strong social relationships provide emotional support, belonging, and a feeling of connection, which improves general well-being.

Promoting Physical and Mental Health:
Happiness and well-being are dependent on both physical and mental health. Prioritize self-care methods that enhance physical vitality, such as regular exercise, a healthy diet, enough sleep, and stress management skills. Similarly, prioritize your mental health by practicing mindfulness, meditation, self-reflection, and getting professional help when necessary. A strong mind-body connection is essential for happiness and resilience in the face of life's adversities.

Discovering Meaning and Purpose:
Living a purpose-driven life is essential for long-term pleasure and contentment. Discover the hobbies, interests, and endeavors that give your life meaning and purpose. Participate in activities that reflect your beliefs, interests, and abilities, such as volunteering, artistic expression, pursuing hobbies, or contributing to issues you care about. Finding meaning in your everyday activities promotes a feeling of pleasure and happiness that goes beyond worldly affluence.

Cultivating gratitude and appreciation:
Practicing thankfulness is an effective strategy to promote pleasure and well-being in your life. Take time each day to focus on the gifts, joys, and possibilities in your life, and show appreciation for the small pleasures and experiences that make you happy. Cultivate an attitude of gratitude for the richness in your life, changing your emphasis from what you lack to what you possess. Gratitude encourages a pleasant attitude and increases overall life happiness.

Live in the Present Moment:
Practicing mindfulness and presence is essential for feeling happy and healthy in the present moment. Develop mindfulness activities that help you remain anchored in the present moment, such as meditation, deep breathing, or mindful walking. Let go of regrets from the past and concerns about the future, and instead concentrate on completely participating in the present moment and experiencing the richness of life as it happens.

Embracing Personal Development and Learning:
Continuous personal development and learning provide a feeling of contentment and well-being. Accept possibilities for self-improvement, growth, and learning, whether via formal education, skill development, or exploring new experiences and challenges. Develop a growth attitude, seeing problems as opportunities for learning and progress rather than setbacks or failures.

Connecting with Nature and Outdoors:

Spending time in nature and interacting with the outdoors may boost happiness and well-being. Take the opportunity to immerse oneself in natural areas, whether it's trekking in the mountains, walking along the beach, or just relaxing in a nearby park. Nature has a therapeutic influence on the mind, body, and soul, lowering stress, improving mood, and instilling awe and amazement.

Performing Acts of Kindness and Generosity:

Acts of kindness and charity towards others are effective methods to promote happiness and well-being. Look for ways to give back to your community, assist people in need, or engage in random acts of kindness. Acts of kindness not only help others, but they also provide a feeling of satisfaction, connection, and purpose in your own life.

Conclusion:

Cultivating pleasure and well-being beyond money is critical to having a full and meaningful life. You can improve your overall well-being and experience more joy, fulfillment, and satisfaction in all aspects of your life by cultivating meaningful relationships, nurturing physical and mental health, discovering purpose and meaning, practicing gratitude and mindfulness, embracing personal growth, connecting with nature, and engaging in acts of kindness. Remember that genuine happiness comes from inside and is fostered by deliberate choices, attitudes, and behaviors that emphasize well-being and satisfaction above material possessions.

Crossing The Gap

Chapter 16: Giving Back and Legacy Planning

16.1 The Importance of Giving Back

In a society dominated by selfish interests and aspirations, the act of giving back serves as a beacon of hope, compassion, and unity. In this section, we will look at the significance of giving back to society and the community, emphasizing the transforming power it may have on people, communities, and the world at large.

cultivating a sense of purpose and fulfillment:

Giving back is more than just an altruistic gesture; it leads to personal satisfaction and a feeling of purpose. Individuals may connect with something more than themselves by engaging in acts of charity, compassion, and service, which tap into a higher sense of purpose and satisfaction that goes beyond monetary pursuits. Giving back, whether via volunteer work, charity gifts, or acts of kindness, allows people to make a good impact on the lives of others while also enhancing their own.

Forming Stronger Communities and Societies:

Giving back is really about strengthening communities and society. When people band together to help one another, whether via charity, volunteering, or community activities, they foster a culture of solidarity, compassion, and shared responsibility. Giving back creates the groundwork for a more equal and just world in which everyone has the chance to prosper by addressing the needs of society's most vulnerable people while also developing a sense of belonging and inclusion.

Addressing social and environmental challenges:

Giving back is critical to tackling today's severe social and environmental concerns. Poverty and hunger, as well as climate change and environmental degradation, are all concerns that demand communal action and assistance. Individuals and groups may help to promote social justice, environmental sustainability, and human well-being by contributing to charities, advocating for causes, and launching community-based projects. Philanthropists and change-makers may use their resources, knowledge, and influence to promote good change and build a better future for future generations.

Inspire others and create a ripple effect:

One of the most powerful parts of giving back is the capacity to inspire others and create a chain reaction of compassion and generosity. When people see acts of compassion and service, they are frequently encouraged to pay it forward by spreading love and goodwill to others in their communities and beyond. Individuals who lead by example and demonstrate the benefits of giving back may start a chain reaction of good change that spreads far and wide, creating a lasting legacy of compassion, empathy, and social responsibility.

Developing a Culture of Gratitude and Appreciation:

Giving back promotes a culture of gratitude and appreciation by reminding people of their gifts and privileges and motivating them to share their wealth with others. When people give back to others in need, they develop empathy and compassion, understanding their connectivity with the rest of the human family. Individuals may foster a more compassionate and fair society by showing appreciation for what they have and sharing their resources with others, ensuring that everyone's fundamental needs are addressed and that everyone has the chance to develop.

Leaving a Permanent Legacy of Impact and Meaning:

Finally, giving back helps people leave a lasting legacy of effect and significance that extends beyond their own lives and benefits future generations. Individuals may contribute to organizations they care about by making charitable gifts, volunteering, or advocating for them, leaving a legacy of compassion, generosity, and social change. Individuals may guarantee that their contributions make a difference long after they are gone by aligning their activities with their beliefs and investing in projects that have a long-term effect, leaving behind a world that is brighter, fairer, and more compassionate than when they arrived.

Conclusion:

In conclusion, the value of giving back cannot be overemphasized. Giving back is a powerful force for positive change in the world, ranging from promoting personal satisfaction and strengthening communities to tackling social and environmental issues and leaving a lasting legacy of influence and purpose. Individuals who embrace a spirit of generosity, compassion, and service may make a significant impact in the lives of others while also contributing to a more fair, equitable, and sustainable world for everyone. As we continue on the road of giving back, let us recall Mahatma Gandhi's famous quote, "The best way to find yourself is to lose yourself in the service of others."

16.2 Plan Your Legacy and Impact

As we go through life, it's natural to think about the legacy we'll leave behind: the influence we'll have on future generations and the imprint we'll make on the world. Legacy planning is the purposeful and intentional process of identifying and molding the legacy we want to leave behind, ensuring that our values, beliefs, and accomplishments are remembered long after we are gone. In this section, we'll examine the significance of legacy planning and provide practical advice on how to plan your legacy and influence.

Understanding Legacy Planning:

Legacy planning is the act of expressing your future beliefs, objectives, and ambitions, as well as making deliberate efforts to guarantee that your legacy represents them. It entails defining the values and causes that are most important to you, deciding how you want to be remembered, and developing a strategy for achieving your legacy objectives. Legacy planning includes a variety of topics, such as financial preparation, estate planning, charity giving, and philanthropic efforts, all to leave a lasting effect on the world.

Reflection on Your Values and Beliefs:

The first stage in legacy planning is to consider your underlying values, beliefs, and principles, which influence your life and worldview. What's most important to you? What issues are you most enthusiastic about? What type of influence do you want to have on the world? Take the time to reflect and determine the values and causes that are most important to you, since they will serve as the basis for your legacy planning efforts.

Specifying Your Legacy Goals:

After you've defined your basic principles and beliefs, define your legacy goals: the specific results and influence you hope to achieve through your legacy. Are you looking to make a difference in your community? Support causes that are consistent with your values. Generate opportunities for future generations. Make an impact in your area or industry. Define your legacy objectives clearly and specifically, ensuring that they represent your greatest dreams and wishes for the future.

Estate planning and wealth transfers:

Estate planning is an important part of legacy planning because it ensures that your assets and money are passed as you intend and utilized to support your legacy objectives. Collaborate with estate planning experts, such as lawyers and financial advisers, to develop a complete estate plan that includes a will, trusts, beneficiary designations, and other legal papers. Consider how you might utilize your financial resources to help you achieve your legacy objectives, whether via charity bequests, endowments, or other planned giving methods.

Charitable giving and philanthropy:

Charitable giving is an effective way to have a long-term influence on the issues and organizations that are important to you. Consider creating a donor-advised fund, foundation, or charitable trust to support philanthropic organizations and activities that are consistent with your beliefs and legacy intentions. Investigate options for strategic philanthropy, which focuses your giving on areas where you can have the biggest effect and generate real change. Involve your family and loved ones in your charitable endeavors, creating a culture of giving and service that will last for decades.

Developing a Family Legacy Plan:

In addition to your legacy plan, consider developing a family legacy plan that involves your loved ones in the process of defining and molding your family's legacy. Hold family gatherings or retreats to discuss your family's beliefs, customs, and goals for the future. Involve family members in decision-making processes regarding charity giving, asset transfer, and legacy planning to ensure that your family's legacy represents its members' collective beliefs and ambitions.

Documenting your legacy:

Documenting your legacy is an important step in preserving your ideals, beliefs, and life experiences for future generations. Consider drafting a legacy letter or book that captures your life narrative, beliefs, and knowledge to pass on to your family. Create a digital library of photographs, films, and keepsakes that highlight significant events and milestones in your life. Consider using technology and storytelling to share your legacy with future generations in meaningful and impactful ways.

Evaluating your impact:

Regularly assess your effect and progress toward your legacy objectives, making modifications as appropriate to ensure that your efforts are consistent with your beliefs and ambitions. Monitor the results of your charity contributions and philanthropic projects to determine the impact you're having in the community and around the world. Celebrate your triumphs, learn from your mistakes, and keep your legacy planning strategy open and adaptable.

Seeking professional guidance

Legacy planning may be difficult and varied, involving knowledge of estate planning, tax law, charity, and asset management. Seek help from skilled specialists, such as estate planning lawyers, financial advisers, and charitable consultants, who may give specialized advice and assistance based on your specific requirements and circumstances. Working with a team of specialists, you may develop a complete legacy plan that matches your current beliefs, objectives, and future ambitions.

Conclusion:

Legacy planning is a significant effort in which people may determine their long-term effects on the planet and future generations. By meditating on your beliefs, establishing your legacy objectives, participating in strategic philanthropy, including your loved ones, recording your legacy, and getting expert advice, you may construct a legacy plan that represents your greatest hopes and wants for the future. Remember that your legacy is more than simply the things you leave behind; it is also about the people you touch, the values you implant, and the influence you have on the world. As you begin the road of legacy planning, may you be motivated to leave a legacy of love, compassion, and enduring importance that will be remembered for years?

16.3 Building a Lasting Financial Legacy

Leaving a financial legacy is more than simply acquiring money; it is about leveraging your financial resources to positively influence the globe and future generations. In this part, we will look at how to create a financial legacy that represents your beliefs, supports your charitable aims, and has a long-term influence on the world.

Defining your financial legacy:

Before you can establish a long-term financial legacy, you must first identify what that legacy means for you. Consider your values, beliefs, and future goals. What issues are you most enthusiastic about? What influence do you want to have on the world? Clarifying your financial legacy objectives allows you to create a plan for achieving them.

Strategic Philanthropy:

Strategic donations are one of the most successful strategies to leave a long-term financial legacy. Strategic philanthropy is carefully planning and directing charity gifts to optimize their effect. Consider directing your charitable contributions toward issues that match your beliefs and interests, such as education, healthcare, environmental protection, and social justice. By wisely directing your donations, you can make a significant impact in the areas that matter most to you.

Establish a Charitable Foundation:

Establishing a nonprofit foundation may be a great way to have a long-term effect. Over time, a charitable foundation allows you to combine your assets and make gifts to charity organizations and projects. By establishing an endowment inside the foundation, you may guarantee that your philanthropic contribution continues indefinitely, providing a legacy for future generations. Charitable foundations also provide flexibility and control over how your money is spent, enabling you to customize your donation to changing needs and priorities.

Endowment Scholarships and Grants:

Another approach to leaving a financial legacy is to fund scholarships and grants that promote education and opportunity. By providing scholarships for worthy students or grants for budding entrepreneurs, artists, or researchers, you may provide people access to knowledge and resources that can improve their lives and affect the future. Endowed scholarships and grants may benefit recipients for decades, allowing them to pursue their goals and make a positive difference in their communities and beyond.

Legacy gifts and bequests:

Incorporating charity bequests and legacy donations into your estate plan is an effective way to leave a lasting financial legacy. Designating a part of your assets to charity causes and organizations allows you to support causes that are important to you even after you are gone. Legacy gifts may take numerous forms, such as cash, stocks, real estate, or other assets. By including charity bequests in your will or trust, you may guarantee that your philanthropic legacy continues, having a long-term influence on the causes and communities you care about.

Impact Investment:

Impact investing is a novel strategy for driving social and environmental change while earning financial gains. Impact investors may align their financial ambitions with their beliefs and priorities by investing in businesses, funds, or initiatives that have positive social and environmental effects. Impact investing enables you to use your financial resources to tackle urgent social and environmental issues, including poverty, inequality, climate change, and sustainable development. Investing in impact-driven companies allows you to make a good difference in the world while also possibly receiving a financial return.

Activating Family and Loved Ones:

Leaving a lasting financial legacy entail not just what you do with your money but also the values you establish for future generations. Engage your family and loved ones in discussions about your charitable objectives, beliefs, and priorities. Encourage an open discussion about the value of giving back and the influence your family can have on the world. Involving your family in your charitable activities may teach a sense of duty, compassion, and social conscience that will last for future generations.

Professional Advice and Support:

Leaving a lasting financial legacy may be complicated and multidimensional, requiring careful preparation, smart decision-making, and professional advice. Work with financial experts, estate planners, and charitable consultants to create a complete legacy plan that is personalized to your specific objectives and values. Using their experience and insights, you can confidently navigate the complexity of legacy planning, ensuring that your financial legacy matches your greatest hopes and objectives for the future.

Conclusion:

Leaving a financial legacy is a significant activity that enables you to positively affect the planet and future generations. You can leave a lasting impact on the world by defining your financial legacy goals, engaging in strategic philanthropy, establishing charitable foundations, endowing scholarships and grants, including legacy gifts in your estate plan, involving family and loved ones, and seeking professional guidance and support. As you embark on the road to establishing a lasting financial legacy, may you be encouraged to utilize your financial resources to make a significant impact on the world and leave a legacy for future generations?

Crossing The Gap

Conclusion

As we near the conclusion of this thorough guide to building financial stamina, it's important to reflect on the trip we've taken and the useful insights we've gathered along the way. Throughout this book, we've covered a variety of subjects, from defining financial freedom to legacy planning, all to empower you to take charge of your financial future and achieve long-term success.

At the center of our investigation is the notion of financial freedom: the opportunity to live life on your terms, free of financial stress and uncertainty. We've looked into what financial independence means, and we've discovered that it's about more than simply accumulating money; it's about gaining a feeling of stability, flexibility, and peace of mind in your finances.

We've also looked at the significance of defining clear financial goals, connecting your beliefs with your spending and saving habits, and developing a plan for reaching your long-term objectives. Understanding your present financial condition, determining your objectives, and applying smart budgeting, saving, and investing techniques can help you chart a road to better financial stability and success.

Throughout our conversations on debt management, emergency reserves, investment, retirement planning, and other topics, one recurring theme has emerged: the need to approach financial management proactively and deliberately. Whether you're paying off debt, developing an investing portfolio, or saving for retirement, every financial choice you make can define your future and determine your degree of financial security.

We've also stressed the need to give back and leave a good legacy, not just for yourself but for future generations. By embracing philanthropy, strategic giving, and legacy planning, you may leave a lasting impression on the world and guarantee that your beliefs and goals live on long after you are gone.

As you continue on your path to financial stamina, keep in mind that it's not only about getting there but also about enjoying the process and the route. Take time to enjoy your accomplishments, learn from your setbacks, and stay focused on your financial goals and objectives.

Finally, I urge you to utilize the information and insights obtained from this book in your own life, making decisive efforts to improve your financial foundation and create the future you want. By arming yourself with the means, resources, and mentality required to attain financial independence, you may live a life of plenty, satisfaction, and success for yourself and the people you care about.

Thank you for joining me on this journey, and may your road to financial strength be filled with success, progress, and joy.

Glossary

Navigating the world of finance may be like learning a new language, complete with its vocabulary and jargon. This dictionary defines major financial terminology used in personal finance, investing, and wealth management, allowing you to better comprehend and analyze financial information.

1. Assets:

Assets are valuable stuff that you possess, including cash, investments, real estate, and personal property. Assets are often classified as liquid (easy to convert into cash) or non-liquid.

2. Liabilities:

Liabilities refer to financial commitments or debts owed to others, such as loans, mortgages, or credit card bills. Liabilities are claims against your assets that are often defined as short-term (due within one year) or long-term (due more than one year).

3. Net worth:

Net worth is calculated as the difference between your total assets and liabilities. It shows your whole financial situation and is a measure of your wealth or financial health. A positive net worth shows that your assets outnumber your obligations, while a negative net worth suggests the reverse.

4. Budget:

A budget is a financial plan that specifies your income and expenditures for a specified period, usually monthly or annually. Budgeting allows you to keep track of your spending, prioritize costs, and reach your financial objectives.

5. Compound interest:

Compound interest is the process of generating interest on an investment's principle as well as any prior interest gained. Over time, compound interest may greatly raise the value of an investment, resulting in exponential growth.

6. Diversification:

Diversification is a risk management approach that entails spreading your assets across asset classes, sectors, or geographic locations to mitigate the effect of a single investment on your whole portfolio. Diversification may reduce risk while increasing the potential for long-term gains.

7. Asset Allocation:
Asset allocation is the act of dividing your investing portfolio into several asset classes, such as stocks, bonds, and cash, depending on your risk tolerance, investment objectives, and time horizon. Asset allocation is a major factor influencing portfolio performance and risk.

8. Mutual Funds:
A mutual fund is a kind of investment instrument that combines funds from different participants and invests them in a diverse portfolio of stocks, bonds, and other assets. Mutual funds are managed by experienced fund managers and provide clients with a simple option to diversify their assets.

9. Exchange-traded fund (ETF):
An exchange-traded fund (ETF) is a sort of investment fund that trades on stock exchanges, like individual equities. ETFs usually replicate an index or benchmark and provide investors with a diverse portfolio of assets at a cheaper cost than conventional mutual funds.

10. Stock:
A stock, also known as a share or equity, is a unit of ownership in a firm. When you acquire stock, you become a shareholder and get a percentage of the company's assets and profits. Stocks are exchanged on stock exchanges and may provide investors with both capital appreciation and dividend income.

11. Bond:
A bond is a fixed-income instrument that reflects a loan from an investor to a government or enterprise. Bonds normally pay out periodic interest payments, known as coupons, and refund the principal amount at maturity. Bonds are typically considered lower-risk investments than stocks, although they have lesser potential profits.

12. Retirement Accounts:
A retirement account is a tax-advantaged investment account used to help people save for retirement. Common retirement accounts include 401(k) plans, individual retirement accounts (IRAs), and Roth IRAs. Contributions to retirement funds might be tax-deductible or tax-deferred, depending on the kind of account.

13. Financial Advisor:
A financial adviser is an expert who offers financial advice and direction to individuals, families, and enterprises. Financial advisers may assist customers with several elements of financial planning, such as retirement planning, investment management, tax planning, and estate planning.

14. Credit score:

A credit score is a numerical estimate of a person's creditworthiness based on their credit history and financial behavior. Lenders use credit scores to evaluate the risk of lending money to borrowers and to set credit conditions such as interest rates and loan amounts.

15. Inflation:

Inflation is the rate at which the overall level of prices for goods and services grows over time, resulting in a reduction in buying power. Inflation gradually erodes money's value, affecting investment returns and the cost of living.

Conclusion:

This dictionary is a great resource for navigating the complicated world of finance and better understanding the language used in personal finance, investing, and asset management. By becoming acquainted with this essential financial terminology, you may improve your financial literacy, make educated choices, and reach your financial objectives with confidence.